Contents

Content guidance

Questions & Answers

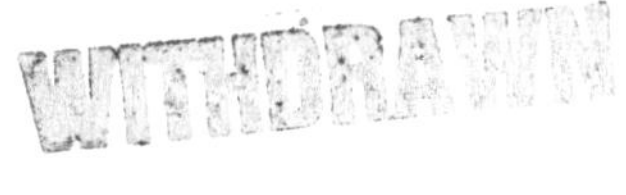

Getting the most from this book

Examiner tips

Advice from the examiner on key points in the text to help you learn and recall unit content, avoid pitfalls, and polish your exam technique in order to boost your grade.

Knowledge check

Rapid-fire questions throughout the Content guidance section to check your understanding.

Knowledge check answers

1 Turn to the back of the book for the Knowledge check answers.

Summary

Summaries

- Each core topic is rounded off by a bullet-list summary for quick-check reference of what you need to know.

Questions & Answers

Exam-style questions

Examiner comments on the questions
Tips on what you need to do to gain full marks, indicated by the icon ⓔ.

Sample student answers
Practise the questions, then look at the student answers that follow each set of questions.

Cognitive psychology | Question 3

(d) Describe and evaluate research into the multi-store model of memory. (10 marks)

ⓔ This is not as straightforward as it might first appear. It is a question on the multi-store model, but on careful reading it should be clear that the emphasis of the question is on 'research'. You are expected to show your knowledge of research by offering a clear description of relevant studies, and this knowledge and description is worth half of the marks. The remaining marks are for evaluation, i.e. presenting strengths and limitations of the studies. These marks can be gained by explaining how well the research supports the model. Alternative models can be referred to but must be made relevant to the question. Simply describing and evaluating the multi-store model without reference to research will not be creditworthy.

Total: 20 marks

Student A

(a) Sunayna might be getting interference between the French she has already learned and the new language **a**.

ⓔ **1/2 marks awarded. a** The student has correctly identified an appropriate theory of forgetting but the answer is brief and does not really explain how the interference might occur. For example, the student could say that there is proactive interference because the French language she has already learned may be coming forward and interfering with the Spanish that she is attempting to learn now.

(b) Studies into interference have usually been experiments and these lack ecological validity **a**.

ⓔ **1/2 marks awarded. a** Here the student has made two points, both of which are valid and could refer to interference theory, but the criticism is not fully outlined. Why experiments lack ecological validity is not explained, and therefore it is not clear why this is a criticism.

(c) (i) The independent variable is the level of processing (whether it is deep or shallow) **a**. The dependent variable is the words **b**.

ⓔ **1/2 marks awarded.** This answer is not sufficient to gain the full 2 marks. **a** The IV is sufficiently clearly stated, but the **b** DV is too vague for a mark. Remember to state exactly what it is that will be measured.

(ii) This is a repeated measures design **c**. This is because the same participants are doing both the shallow processing and the deep processing condition **d**. This design is good because you do not have any individual differences, but the problem is counterbalancing **e**.

ⓔ **2/2 marks awarded.** This answer gets the full 2 marks for correctly **c** naming and **d** explaining the relevant design. However, **e** the last sentence is redundant because the question does not ask for any evaluation.

Unit 2: Social Psychology, Cognitive Psychology and Individual Differences 65

Examiner commentary on sample student answers
Find out how many marks each answer would be awarded in the exam and then read the examiner comments (preceded by the icon ⓔ) following each student answer. Annotations that link back to points made in the student answers show exactly how and where marks are gained or lost.

About this book

This is a guide to Unit 2 of the AQA(B) AS Psychology specification. It is intended as a revision aid rather than as a textbook. Its purpose is to summarise the content, to explain how the content will be assessed, to look at the type of questions to expect and to consider specimen answers.

There are six topic areas in Unit 2 and you have to answer questions on three of these topics in your examination. You must answer questions on one topic in social psychology, one on cognitive psychology and one on individual differences. The choice of topics is as follows:

Social influence	**OR**	Social cognition
Remembering and forgetting	**OR**	Perceptual processes
Anxiety disorders	**OR**	Autism

For each of these topics, this guide will cover the following:

- the specification content, which tells you exactly what you need to know and learn
- appropriate content relevant to the topic. This gives you minimal coverage of the topic, the details of which you should already have learned in your studies. The focus is on key terms and concepts, main theories and studies, and evaluation points. The content here is not the only material you should consider: textbooks will cover the topics in various ways and give much more detail as well as alternative studies.
- a sample question in the style of AQA(B) AS questions, similar to those that you might expect to see on real examination papers
- an analysis of how the question should be tackled and what the examiners are looking for in an answer
- a typical grade-C/D student answer (student A), together with examiner comments showing where the marks have been gained and lost, drawing attention to any errors and giving suggestions as to how the answers might be improved or elaborated to get extra marks
- a typical grade-A student answer (student B), followed by examiner comments that show which points are especially creditworthy. If you read these sample answers and comments carefully, you will learn a lot about what you need to do to present a really effective answer in the examination.

How to use this guide

First, check your class notes and revision notes against the content presented here to make sure that you have all the right material for your revision. Then look at a sample question to see how the exam is structured and what is required. Try to answer the question, then examine the sample answers and comments to see where credit can be gained and lost. The sample answers are not intended as model answers but as tools to help you understand what makes a good answer. Finally, you should review your own answer in the light of what you have read and consider how your own response to the question might be improved.

Content guidance

In this section, content guidance is offered on the topic areas of social psychology, cognitive psychology and individual differences. Each topic begins with a summary of the AQA Specification B requirements for Unit 2. This is followed by a brief account of the theories and studies that make up the unit content.

Knowledge of appropriate theories and studies is essential for the AS examination. It is also important to be able to assess their value, and this is done here with regular 'Evaluation' features that provide criticisms of both.

Names and publication dates have been given when referring to research studies. The full details for these studies are normally available in textbooks, should you wish to research the topic further.

Social psychology

Social influence

Social facilitation

Summary specification content

Social facilitation, dominant responses, causes of arousal: evaluation apprehension and distraction. Effects of arousal on task performance.

Examiner tip
Make sure you have a brief, accurate definition of the key terms on the specification, including: social facilitation; dominant responses; evaluation apprehension and distraction.

Inhibit To hinder or decrease.

Social facilitation is concerned with how and why activity is increased (**facilitated**) when others are present. For example, athletes run faster if an **audience** is watching, and even cockroaches learn to navigate a maze faster if watched by other roaches. **Coaction effects** refer to the presence of others independently carrying out the same task at the same time, which usually facilitates performance. Triplett (1898) found that cyclists rode faster when racing with others, and that children could reel a fishing line faster in pairs than when on their own. The presence of others seems to enhance performance, but this is true only of well-learned or automatic behaviours. Studies have shown that the presence of others can inhibit behaviour that is not well learned or is complex.

Study: Schmitt et al. (1986)

Schmitt et al. requested participants to perform two tasks: (a) an easy task, typing their name into a computer; (b) a difficult task, typing their name backwards, with numbers inserted between each letter. An audience facilitated performance on the easy task but inhibited performance on the difficult task. This study showed that **task difficulty** determined whether an audience facilitated or inhibited performance.

To explain how spectators can facilitate performance on some tasks but inhibit it on others, Zajonc (1965) proposed a **drive theory of social facilitation**. He suggested that spectators create an innate response in performers, known as '**arousal**', which prepares a person to respond. The presence of others increases arousal, which increases a person's tendency to perform **dominant responses**. Dominant responses refer to the behaviour that we are most likely to perform in a given situation. If a person is highly skilled, his or her dominant response will be to perform well, and this accurate behaviour will be facilitated by spectators. When someone is learning a new skill, the dominant response will be to make errors, and his or her performance will be inhibited by spectators.

Knowledge check 1

Explain how a dominant response can either hinder or facilitate performance on a task.

The **Yerkes–Dodson Law** predicts an inverted U-shaped function between arousal and performance. It suggests that as arousal increases, performance increases, but that a point is reached where increased arousal leads to a *decrease* in performance. Different tasks necessitate different levels of arousal, and there is an optimal level for each task. For example, tasks that require a lot of concentration may call for a lower level of arousal, whereas tasks that demand stamina may necessitate higher levels of arousal.

There are two distinct factors to the Yerkes-Dodson Law: the upward portion of the inverted 'U' is the positive effect of arousal, while the downward part is the negative effect of arousal. The highest point of the 'U' shape is the optimal level of arousal for that task (see Figure 1).

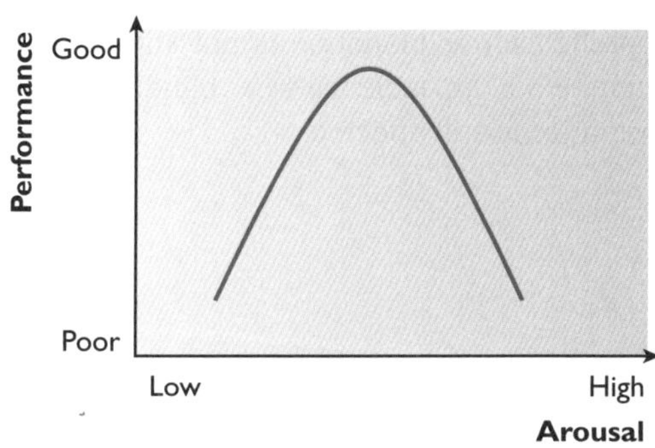

Figure 1 The Yerkes–Dodson inverted 'U'

Knowledge check 2

Think of a personal example of where evaluation apprehension has occurred and whether this facilitated or inhibited your performance.

Evaluation apprehension was proposed by Cottrell (1972) to explain how, when we are in the presence of other people, we are concerned that they may be judging us. When we think that someone is evaluating our performance, arousal occurs and a well-learned task can be enhanced. However, on a difficult task, arousal may be too high and performance inhibited.

Examiner tip

When trying to understand and learn studies, think about how they have been devised, thus practising 'how science works'. Think about the aim/hypothesis of each study and the design employed, e.g. is it a repeated measures or independent groups design experiment? Also, consider the independent and dependent variables, the sample and any controls, and so on.

Study: Baris et al. (1988)

Evaluation apprehension was investigated by Baris et al. One group of participants had to think of as many different uses for a knife as possible, while a second group had to think only of creative uses for a knife. Half the participants in each group were told that their performance would be collected together as a group, while the other half in each group were in the 'evaluation apprehension condition' and were told that their individual performance would be identified. Participants in the 'evaluation apprehension condition' performed less well on the complex task requiring creativity but were superior on the simpler task of identifying uses for a knife. This showed that evaluation apprehension facilitated performance on a simple task but inhibited performance on a complex task.

Baron (1986) has proposed an alternative explanation for social facilitation: the **distraction-conflict model**. Other people present when a task is being performed can be distracting, and some attention is lost from the task. A **response conflict** occurs between attending to the task and the audience, which has a negative effect on task performance. At the same time, response conflict increases arousal, leading to a **dominant response**, which facilitates performance on a simple task but inhibits performance of a more difficult task. The negative effects of distraction outweigh the positive effects of arousal and motivation on difficult tasks.

Dominant response The behaviour that we are most likely to perform in a given situation.

Evaluation

- The tasks that the participants perform in studies of social facilitation are often artificial and may lack ecological validity.
- Audiences in studies of social facilitation are usually quiet, and therefore may not reflect the nature of audiences or co-actors in the real world.
- The evaluation apprehension explanation is not supported by studies that show how, even when members of an audience wear blindfolds and are therefore unable to judge, the performance is still affected.

Examiner tip

Make sure you have a brief, accurate definition of the key terms on the specification, including: internalisation, compliance, informational social influence and normative social influence, and be careful not to confuse *types* with *explanations*, as these two words often appear in questions.

Conformity

Summary specification content

Types of conformity, including internalisation and compliance. Explanations for conformity, including informational social influence and normative social influence. Factors affecting conformity, including those investigated by Asch.

Conformity has been defined by Crutchfield (1955) as 'yielding to group pressure', and this pressure can be real or imagined. Conformity is more likely to occur in groups that are important to an individual, such as **membership groups**, which include family members and peers, and **reference groups**, which are those to which we would like to belong.

Knowledge check 3

Use an example to distinguish between 'compliance' and 'internalisation'.

Types of conformity

- **Compliance**: publicly going along with the group opinion, but privately disagreeing and maintaining our own beliefs.
- **Internalisation**: going along with the group opinion both privately and publicly.

Explanations for conformity

Informational social influence

When we conform because we do not know the answer or how to react, this is **informational social influence**. In ambiguous situations, we look to others for information. This type of influence usually results in internalisation and adoption of the views and behaviours of others.

Informational social influence Conforming to the majority view due to new information/reasoning; this results in both public and private acceptance of the view.

Study: Sherif (1935)

Sherif carried out a study using the **autokinetic effect** (a visual illusion where a stationary light in a darkened room appears to move). He asked participants to estimate how far the light had moved. Each participant did this individually over a series of trials so that an average could be calculated for each of them. Participants were then divided into groups, including people with very different averages, and again asked to make individual judgements in the group situation. After a few trials carried out in groups, individual judgements tended to move towards the group norm. This effect was still evident when the tests were repeated later, with participants being tested individually. Participants appear to have conformed in this situation because they were uncertain of the 'correct' answer.

Examiner tip

Think critically about studies that you read so that you can discuss evidence more fully in the examination. One problem with the Sherif (1935) study is that there was no 'correct answer', as the light did not actually move! Often, criticisms of studies lead to further research, which you can then discuss, for example, as in this case the Asch (1956) study.

Normative social influence

Normative social influence is an explanation for conformity based on the need to be the same as other people and accepted by other people. This links to the type of conformity known as **compliance**. Sometimes we go along with a group decision, even though we do not agree with it, because we want to be part of that group and do not want to be ridiculed or rejected.

Normative social influence Conforming to the majority view in order to be accepted/approved by others, in order not to be different; this results in public acceptance of the view.

Study: Asch (1956)

Asch devised a conformity task that was **unambiguous**. Participants had to compare the length of a vertical line (X) with three other lines, one of which was clearly the same length as X. People were seated around a table and answered one at a time. There was only one real participant, who was last but one to answer. All the other people were confederates who had been 'primed' to give the wrong answer on some of the trials. The results showed an overall conformity rate of 32%, with 74% conforming on at least one trial. Conformity occurred even though participants could clearly see that the answer was wrong.

Unambiguous Not confusing or misleading — where there is no doubt.

Factors affecting conformity (Asch)

- **Task difficulty**. When the task was made more difficult by making the comparison lines more similar, conformity levels increased.
- **Unanimity**. If one of the confederates gave the correct answer, conformity decreased dramatically, to just 5%. In the presence of an ally, the real participant was more confident about giving the right answer.
- **Answering in private**. When participants were able to give their answers in private, conformity dropped to 12.5%.

Examiner tip

Questions often ask about *factors*. You are required to know some of the factors affecting conformity as investigated by Asch. Make sure you understand whether the factor under discussion increases or decreases conformity.

Knowledge check 4

Identify and outline:

(i) one factor that leads to an increase in conformity

(ii) one factor that leads to a decrease in conformity.

- **Size of the majority**. Asch found that conformity increased as the number of confederates increased:

	Conformity %
One real participant and one confederate	0
One real participant and two confederates	14
One real participant and three confederates	32

After three confederates, conformity levels stayed the same.

Obedience

Summary specification content

Explanations of obedience. Situational factors: conditions affecting obedience to authority as investigated by Milgram. Dispositional explanation: the authoritarian personality. Explanations of defiance of authority. Ethical and methodological issues in studying social influence.

Obedience is concerned with acting in a particular way because of an order from an **authority figure**. Psychologists have been interested in investigating the reasons why people obey orders from an authority figure, and explanations concern either factors about the situation that lead to obedience or factors within the individual.

Examiner tip

Make sure you have a brief, accurate definition of the key terms on the specification, including: situational and dispositional factors, authoritarian personality, defiance of authority.

Situational factors to explain why people obey orders

Milgram investigated a number of situational factors that affected obedience to authority.

Examiner tip

Take care that you understand the difference between conformity and obedience. Students sometimes confuse these in the examination. Obedience always involves an authority figure.

Study: Milgram (1963)

Participants had responded to a newspaper advertisement to take part in a study supposedly on learning, for which they would be paid $4.50. The study took place at Yale University. There was an experimenter in a laboratory coat, a 'learner' (who was a confederate) and a 'teacher' (the only real participant) who had to administer an 'electric shock'. The size of the shock was to be increased by moving one point up the 15- to 400-volt scale each time the learner gave an incorrect answer. No electric shocks were actually administered, but the experiment was set up in such a way that the teacher thought that electric shocks were being given. The experiment was to test how far the teacher would go in obeying an authority figure. Every teacher went up to 300 volts, and 65% of participants went to the full 450 volts in spite of screams, protestations etc. from the learner.

Examiner tip

Make sure you can describe Milgram's obedience experiment(s) briefly and accurately. Students who write overlong descriptions of the original Milgram experiment in essays can gain only limited knowledge marks and, therefore, waste a lot of time.

Factors in Milgram's study

- **The credibility of the set-up**. Perhaps participants were aware that the learner received no electric shock, i.e. the set-up was not credible. However, this is unlikely because in a study where participants had to give real electric shocks to puppies, obedience was 75% (Sheridan and King 1972).

- **Demand characteristics**. Participants in an experimental setting often respond in the way they do because they want to 'please' the experimenter (or mess up the study), but in the real world they might respond differently. However, studies carried out in a 'real-life setting' with nurses in a hospital showed even higher rates of obedience (Hofling 1966).
- **The perception of legitimate authority**. The **location** (Yale University) added legitimate power, and obedience did decrease when the location changed. The experimenter represented legitimate authority as he was a scientist with a **laboratory coat**, representing the power of the uniform. Bickman (1974) found obedience was even higher when a guard's uniform was worn.

Examiner tip

Read the question carefully in the examination. If the question is on 'factors affecting obedience' then you should restrict your answer to such factors and clearly state whether each factor increases or decreases obedience. Ensure that any discussion of methodology/ethics is linked to the factors.

Dispositional factors to explain why people obey orders

Adorno et al. (1950) proposed that a particular personality type known as the **authoritarian personality** was responsible for increased obedience in an individual. This personality type is rigid, i.e. not open to change and has difficulty coping in situations where there is no right or wrong answer. The authoritarian personality type also shows a particular trait known as '**authoritarian submissiveness**', which makes the person blindly obedient to authority.

Adorno et al. developed a scale for measuring authoritarianism, which became known as the **F-scale**, where 'F' stands for 'Fascism', because authoritarian personality types have extreme right-wing political views. Examples of F-scale statements are: 'Any good leader should be strict with people under him in order to gain respect', 'Obedience and respect for authority are the most important virtues that children should learn'.

Knowledge check 5

Identify and outline one dispositional factor that affects levels of obedience.

The development of the authoritarian personality was believed to be due to childhood experiences, in particular a harsh upbringing with little affection and punishing parents.

Evaluation

- Adorno used a small sample, so generalisation is difficult.
- The questionnaire could produce response set and response bias, as all the statements are in one direction.
- The F-scale predicts that those with an authoritarian personality are submissive to authority figures and therefore should be more likely to give powerful electric shocks in the Milgram experiment. Milgram (1974) found that high scorers on the F-scale gave significantly stronger shocks than low scorers.

Defiance of authority

When people do not obey an authority figure, there is defiance of authority. Milgram investigated a number of variations to his study and found that the levels of obedience dropped under several situational and social conditions:

- **Location**. Changing location from the prestigious Yale University to a downtown office led to a fall in obedience to 47.5%.
- **Proximity**. When the teacher and learner were in the same room, obedience fell to 40%, and when the teacher had to place the learner's arm on the electric plate, it fell to 30%.

Examiner tip
Make sure you are confident in answering a question (even an essay) on 'defiance of authority'. In your answer to such a question remember to refer to variations that lead to a decrease in obedience, i.e. where people defy authority.

- **Instructions**. Instructions by telephone led to a significant drop in obedience levels, to 20.5%.
- **Social support**. Where others defy orders, we are more confident to do the same.

Study: Milgram (1965)

Milgram carried out a variation of his study to see if social support led to a decrease in obedience. There were three confederates (a learner and two teachers) and the real participant, a third teacher. The three teachers sat together. At 150 volts, one confederate teacher rebelled and refused to go on. The second confederate teacher rebelled at 210 volts. When the first confederate rebelled, 80% of participants continued, but when the second rebelled, 60% defied authority and refused to continue. Only 10% went on to the maximum, showing that social support decreases the tendency to obey an authority figure.

Ethical and methodological issues in studying social influence

Ethics

Many social influence studies conflict with the **British Psychological Society** (BPS) **Code of Ethics and Conduct (2006)**. The following issues conflict with current guidelines:

Code of Ethics and Conduct (2006) Guidelines that govern the activities of practising psychologists (including students) when carrying out research. Devised by the BPS, they cover four main principles: respect; competence; responsibility; integrity.

- **Lack of informed consent**. People did not know what they were really agreeing to when they consented to take part.
- **Deception**. This occurred particularly where confederates were used.
- **Protection from harm**. Some studies were potentially damaging and stressful. For example, in the Asch study, participants looked surprised and stressed when presented with the majority answers. Bogdonoff (1961) found that participants in an Asch-type study had greatly increased stress levels.
- **The right to withdraw**. Milgram's participants often wanted to leave but were pressured to continue.

Methodology

- **Artificial laboratory conditions**. These may tell us little about social influence in real life.
- **Replicability**. Much research was carried out in the 1950s and 1960s, often on male students, so generalisation to the present day and to other types of participants may not be possible.
- **Validity**. This concerns the question, 'Is the research measuring what it is supposed to measure?' For example, in the Milgram study, did people really believe that they were administering electric shocks?

Replicability Whether research can be repeated and produce similar results.

Summary

- Social facilitation explains how and why activity is increased when others are present. Spectators can either facilitate or inhibit performance on a task.
- Zajonc's Drive Theory of social facilitation proposes that the presence of others increases arousal, which in turn increases the use of a dominant response.
- Evaluation apprehension is when we are concerned others may be judging us, which leads to arousal.
- The distraction-conflict model refers to the conflict between attending to the task and the audience. This can result in an increase in arousal and dominant response.
- Conformity refers to the tendency to 'go along with the group'. There are two types of conformity: compliance and internalisation.
- There are two explanations of conformity: informational social influence and normative social influence.
- Asch identified a number of factors affecting conformity.
- Obedience is concerned with acting in a particular way because of an order from an authority figure.
- Milgram investigated a number of situational factors that affected obedience.
- Adorno proposed that a particular personality type known as the 'authoritarian personality' was responsible for increased obedience in an individual.
- When people do not obey an authority figure there is defiance of authority.
- There are a number of ethical and methodological issues in studying social influence.

Social cognition

Impression formation

Summary specification content

Factors affecting impression formation, including social schemas, primacy and recency effects, central traits and stereotyping.

Impression formation is all about how we perceive other people. A number of factors have been found to influence the impressions formed, including social schemas, stereotypes, primacy and recency effects, and central traits.

Impression formation Perceiving other people, assessing their traits and characteristics, establishing an attitude towards them.

Social schemas

A schema is an organised pattern of knowledge or behaviour that is derived from past experience and that we can use to interpret the world around us. Schemas allow us to infer details to make a situation or person more understandable. They allow us to make sense of our social world. Fiske and Taylor (1991) identified four main schema types:

- **Self schemas**. These contain specific characteristics and traits that are central to our self-image.
- **Role schemas**. These hold the expectations that we have about people who hold specific roles in society.
- **Event schemas**. These are scripts that tell us what to expect in a particular setting.
- **Person schemas**. These contain knowledge about people we know. We have a schema for each person we know, which holds concepts about that person and allows us to generate expectations.

Examiner tip

The four factors (social schemas, stereotypes, primacy/recency effects, central traits) are named on the specification and therefore you can be asked about any one of them by name.

Examiner tip
Be careful. Event schemas are not always useful as part of an answer to a question on impression formation as they inform us about situations rather than people. They can be made relevant only if you link event schemas to forming impressions of people.

A schema is a personal belief or expectation about a person or group. If these expectations are similar to other people's beliefs, they are called **stereotypes**.

Stereotypes

A stereotype is a set of beliefs and generalisations — often based on a single characteristic — about a group where all members are believed to be the same. Stereotypes are usually negative, but they can also be positive. People hold stereotypes on gender, age, race, appearance etc. — for example, 'Old people are grumpy', 'People who wear glasses are more intelligent' and so on.

Study: Duncan (1976)

Duncan carried out a study into racial stereotypes. He showed participants a film of two people arguing, with four conditions: a white person pushed a white person; a black person pushed a white person; a white person pushed a black person; a black person pushed a black person. When participants rated the push for 'aggressiveness', the black person was always rated as more aggressive.

Primacy and recency effects

The primacy/recency effect (i.e. what we learn first and last about a person) can bias our impression.

Study: Asch (1946)

Asch demonstrated the primacy effect in an experiment. He gave one group of participants a list of words describing a person: 'intelligent; industrious; impulsive; critical; stubborn; envious', and he gave a second group the same words but in reverse order. Two different impressions were formed, a much more positive rating being given to the first group, showing a strong primacy effect.

Examiner tip
You could be asked an essay question on (just) primacy or recency effects, so ensure you are also familiar with a study showing the recency effect.

A study by Luchins (1957) showed that recency effects occur when there is a time delay between two tasks.

Central traits

Some **traits** are more powerful at influencing impression formation than other traits. Central traits, such as the dimension warm–cold, seem to have a much greater effect than peripheral traits such as polite–blunt.

Trait An enduring characteristic of a person, such as honesty.

Study: Kelley (1950)

Kelley conducted a study where a guest lecturer was described to a group of students as either 'warm' or 'cold' before the lecture. After the lecture, the students rated him on a number of characteristics. The ratings were affected by the prior information, with the 'warm' group rating him as more interesting and more competent than the 'cold' group. The members of the 'warm' group were also observed to be more interactive during the lecture.

Knowledge check 6
Explain why the Kelley study is considered more ecologically valid than the study by Asch (1946).

Evaluation

- Asch's study lacked ecological validity because it was simply a list of adjectives and not a real person, and therefore was not true to real life.
- The bias in impression formation, found in studies into central traits and primacy effects, has implications for real life. For example, during interviews, it is crucial to come across as warm and give a good first impression.
- Social schemas are useful as they allow us to interpret a complex world quickly, but we should be aware that they may lead us to pay attention only to things that we expect and therefore miss other important information.

Attribution

Summary specification content

Concept of attribution: dispositional and situational attributions; attributional biases, including the fundamental attribution error, the actor–observer effect and the self-serving bias.

Attribution is concerned with how we assess the causes and reasons behind other people's behaviour. A distinction is made between dispositional and situational attributions:

- **Dispositional (internal) attributions**. The belief that behaviour is caused by something within the person observed, e.g. his or her personality.
- **Situational (external) attributions**. The belief that behaviour is caused by something outside the person observed, i.e. his or her situation.

A dispositional attribution occurs when we decide that someone's behaviour is due to his or her personality, e.g. the person is late because he or she is lazy or incompetent. A situational attribution occurs when we decide that someone's behaviour is the result of his or her situation, e.g. the person is late because the bus broke down.

Knowledge check 7

Explain why dispositional attributions are known as 'internal' whereas situational attributions are known as 'external'.

Attribution biases

The fundamental attribution error (FAE)

The FAE is the tendency to underestimate the importance of situational factors and overestimate the person's **dispositions** when attributing causes to his or her behaviour. Attributions are in error because the situational forces are often ignored.

Disposition The mental and physical aspects of a person that are considered consistent.

Study: Bierbrauer (1979)

Bierbrauer carried out a study where participants had to estimate the amount of disobedience in a re-enactment of the Milgram study. Participants reported that 80% would refuse to deliver the maximum shock, i.e. they consistently underestimated the extent to which the 'teachers' would yield to situational factors.

Examiner tip
Students sometimes find attributional biases confusing. The fundamental attribution error (FAE) and actor-observer effect should be seen as complementary — with the FAE referring only to the behaviour of others, and the actor-observer concerned with the behaviour of others (like the FAE) and also one's own behaviour. Thus the actor-observer bias extends on the FAE.

Bias Inclined towards a particular conclusion.

Actor–observer effect

Whereas in the fundamental attribution error the observer attributes dispositional causes to another's behaviour, with our own behaviour (the actor) there is a tendency to emphasise **situational** factors.

Study: Nisbett (1973)

Nisbett asked participants to explain why they themselves, and then why their friends, had chosen a particular course of study. The participants explained their own choices as due to situational factors, such as the quality of the course, while they explained their friends' choices as due to dispositional factors.

Self-serving bias

We generally have a **bias** to enhance our own abilities and preserve our self-esteem. For example, if we have done well in an examination, the actor/observer bias would predict that we would emphasise situational factors, e.g. 'It was an easy paper'. However, this is not always the case and we often make a dispositional attribution for success, e.g. 'I worked hard', 'I am intelligent'. It would seem that we have a **self-enhancing bias** for success and a **self-protecting bias** for failure.

Study: Johnson (1964)

Johnson asked teachers to attribute responsibility for the performance of their pupils. Teachers reported themselves as being responsible for improved performance (self-enhancing bias) but poor performance was the responsibility of pupils (self-protecting bias).

Evaluation

- There is empirical evidence for the FAE, but this bias ignores attributions made by the actor about his or her own behaviour.
- There is evidence to suggest that the self-serving bias does occur, but Abramson et al. (1978) found that depressed individuals tended to show the opposite bias — attributing their successes situationally and their failures dispositionally.

Attitudes

Summary specification content

The structure and function of attitudes: cognitive, affective and behavioural components; adaptive, knowledge and ego-expressive functions. Explanations of prejudice, including competition for resources, social identity theory and the authoritarian personality.

An attitude is a particularly difficult concept to define, largely because it is to do with what we think, feel and do. One dictionary definition is: 'An enduring pattern of evaluative responses towards a person, object or issue', but this assumes some kind of consistency between attitude and behaviour that is not always found in real life.

The structural approach to attitudes

Attitudes are often considered to have three components: **a**ffective, **b**ehavioural, **c**ognitive.

- The **affective component** refers to how we feel about an attitude object (e.g. like/dislike).
- The **behavioural component** (sometimes called 'conative') refers to actual behaviour towards the attitude object.
- The **cognitive component** refers to beliefs and opinions about an attitude object.

This three-component model assumes that there is a high degree of consistency between the components of an attitude. For example, a person with a negative attitude towards cats would not like cats, would not have a cat at home and would think that cats spread germs. However, there is some evidence that behaviour does not always correspond to the affective and cognitive components of an attitude.

Study: LaPiere (1934)

LaPiere wrote to a number of American establishments to find out if they would be willing to accept Chinese guests. At the time, there was prejudice against Chinese people in the USA. Of the 128 replies, 91% said that they would not. However, when LaPiere turned up at establishments with a Chinese couple, only one hotel refused them. This shows that there is inconsistency between what people say and what they do.

Examiner tip

Think critically about studies that you read so that you can discuss evidence more fully in the examination. For example, one problem with the LaPiere (1934) study is that there were confounding variables, e.g. LaPiere himself was not Chinese. How might this have confounded the results?

The functional approach to attitudes

This approach looks at what functions attitudes serve.

- The **adaptive** function concerns the need to achieve a desired goal and avoid pain/unpleasantness. We may show a particular attitude in order to be accepted by a social group as we seek approval and social acceptance by others. This function is **hedonistic** as it increases pleasure and avoids punishment.
- The **knowledge** function concerns the need for consistency and control in our world so that we can predict what is likely to happen. It allows us to structure and organise our social world.
- The **ego-expressive** function concerns the need to let other people know our opinion and views, and also the need to know our own mind.

Hedonistic
Pleasure-seeking.

Knowledge check 8

Name three structural components of attitudes.

Evaluation

- The functional approach to attitudes has implications for changing attitudes because once the function that a particular attitude serves is known, changing that attitude is more likely. For example, if an attitude is serving a knowledge function, giving that person new information may change his or her attitude.

Examiner tip

Students sometimes find the functional approach to attitudes quite difficult; try to make sure you understand the 3 identified functions and that you can apply them to examples. Make use of past AS examination papers to test your understanding.

- Measuring attitudes has been made possible by concentrating on the affective component of the structural approach. This has proved simple to measure, can effectively summarise an attitude and may predict behaviour.
- There is some evidence that people say one thing but do another (e.g. LaPiere).
- Questionnaires given to people of different cultures may elicit the ego-defensive function of attitudes. People may not tell you their real attitudes because they need to protect themselves.

Prejudice

Prejudice is considered to have the same three components (**a**ffective, **b**ehavioural and **c**ognitive) found in attitudes. It has been defined by Secord and Backman (1974) as 'an attitude that predisposes a person to think, feel and perceive in favourable or unfavourable ways towards a group or its individual members'. Prejudice can be distinguished from **discrimination**, which is the behaviour that often results from prejudicial attitudes. Prejudice takes different forms, e.g. sexism and racism.

Knowledge check 9

'I am going to work harder next year and keep up my voluntary work. I want to go to medical school.' Explain what function this attitude might be serving.

Study: Davey (1983)

Davey demonstrated prejudice in school children. He asked 500 children to share out sweets between three different ethnic groups: white, West Indian and Asian. All ethnic groups allocated more sweets to their own ethnic group, illustrating prejudice even in school children.

Examiner tip

Three explanations for prejudice are named on the specification (competition for resources, social identity theory and the authoritarian personality) and you should be able to describe, evaluate and refer to evidence for each explanation.

Explanations for prejudice

Authoritarian personality

The **authoritarian personality** is strongly associated with prejudiced attitudes. Adorno et al. (1950) were initially concerned with constructing a scale to measure anti-Semitism, and Sandford (1956) developed a nine-component personality questionnaire, known as the F-scale, to measure authoritarianism. A strong positive correlation has consistently been found between authoritarianism and **ethnocentrism**.

Authoritarian personality A person who seeks, and favours, obedience to authority.

Ethnocentrism Viewing one's own ethnic group as superior.

Evaluation

- A methodological problem with the scales is that response set (the respondent just gets into the habit of responding in the same way) might be operating, as agreement with each item of the scale suggests authoritarianism. (NB The scale should be balanced so that some items are scored in the opposite direction.)
- There are other problems with the concept of authoritarianism because prejudice and ethnocentrism can be more readily explained by other factors such as lack of education.

Competition for resources

Group membership can explain prejudice, particularly when groups become competitive with each other. Such **inter-group** conflict was investigated in a series of experiments by Sherif (1966) with a group of 11–12-year-old boys attending summer school camp in America.

Inter-group Between two or more groups.

Examiner tip

Sherif proposed that prejudice occurs due to 'Competition for resources'; this is also known as 'Realistic conflict theory'.

Study: Sherif (1966)

In the first stage of the study, boys mixed with each other and formed friendships. The boys were then divided into two groups and friendship groups were split. This time, activities were restricted to each group and there was no contact with the other group. A strong sense of group identity developed and new friendships were formed. The members of each group gave their group a name (Rattlers and Eagles) and competitions were arranged between the two groups. There was hostility and open conflict between the two groups, with raids on dormitories, name calling etc. Conflict arose because of the competition for resources, food, prizes etc. Sherif concluded that hostility and discrimination result from inter-group conflict.

Evaluation

- Studies have shown that when there is high unemployment, racism is increased.
- Other studies have found that competition did not lead to hostility and discrimination.
- Competition may be neither a necessary nor a sufficient condition for inter-group conflict and discrimination.

Social identity theory

Tajfel and Turner (1986) proposed that competition was not necessary for inter-group discrimination (as suggested by Sherif) as this could occur simply by being a member of a social group. Social identity theory proposes the following points:

- We strive to maintain a **positive self-image**. This can be achieved through social identity, as a positive social identity enhances self-esteem and a sense of belonging.
- The individual creates a positive social identity by over-valuing the **ingroup** (his or her own group) and devaluing the **outgroup**.
- **Social categorisation** results in social discrimination because people make social comparisons between their own group (ingroup) and outgroups.
- Individuals who have a strong **need for acceptance** by others are more likely to have indistinct personal and social identities. This can result in them being more prejudiced.

Study: Abrams and Hogg (1990)

Abrams and Hogg carried out a series of experiments and found that adolescent decisions are affected by comparison with others whom they perceive as being from the same social category. Such groups act as reference points, with ingroups found to be much more influential than parents, teachers etc., who are seen as outgroups.

Knowledge check 10

Identify two groups that you associate with that would be considered 'reference groups'.

Minimal group experiment People are assigned to a particular group but have no knowledge of the other members of their group and no interaction. Even so, ingroup favouritism and outgroup prejudice can occur.

Evaluation

- Knowledge of ingroups and outgroups has led to more effective health education programmes etc.
- The concept of social identity has been criticised as it implies that prejudice is natural and that racism, for example, can be explained and justified.
- There is empirical evidence for social identity theory from **minimal group experiments**.

Summary

- Impression formation is concerned with how we perceive other people. Factors influencing impressions formed include: social schemas, stereotypes, primacy and recency effects, and central traits.
- Attribution is concerned with how we assess the causes and reasons behind our own and others' behaviour. A distinction is made between dispositional and situational attributions.
- There are three attributional biases: (i) the fundamental attribution error (FAE); (ii) the actor-observer effect; (iii) the self-serving bias.
- According to the structural approach, there are three components to attitudes: (i) affective component; (ii) behavioural component; (iii) cognitive component.
- The functional approach to attitudes considers the functions attitudes serve: (i) adaptive; (ii) knowledge; (iii) ego-expressive. Knowledge of the function can lead to attitude change.
- One explanation for prejudice is the authoritarian personality, which can be measured using the 'F' scale.
- Group membership can also explain prejudice, which was investigated in a series of experiments by Sherif (1966).
- Tajfel proposed a social identity theory to explain prejudice.

Cognitive psychology

Remembering and forgetting

Models of memory

Summary specification content

Models of memory, including the distinguishing features/components of each of the following: the multi-store model (Atkinson and Shiffrin); the working memory model; levels of processing. Types of long-term memory: episodic; semantic; procedural.

It is useful to think of memory as consisting of three stages or processes:

- **Encoding**. This refers to the initial registration of information into memory and its conversion into a form or code that will allow storage to occur.

- **Storage** (or **retention**). Memories are held for a period of time, and several theories have emerged as to how these stores are structured and what processes are required to store the memories.
- **Retrieval**. This is the ability to access the stored memories when needed.

There are three models (or theories) of memory named on the specification and you must know, for **each** of these:

(1) the distinguishing features/components
(2) research evidence (studies)
(3) evaluation

The multi-store model of memory (MSM)

The multi-store model of memory (Atkinson and Shiffrin, 1968) distinguishes between the **structural components** of a **short-term memory** store and a **long-term memory** store, and memory processes such as **rehearsal** and **coding**. Rehearsal is considered essential for the transfer of information from short-term memory to long-term memory.

- **Sensory memory (SM) or sensory register**. It holds information for a brief time in the same sense as the one through which the information entered the sensory system, e.g. a visual image is held as a picture. Sperling (1960) carried out a series of experiments and found that sensory memory holds information for only a brief period of time (less than a second).
- **Short-term memory (STM)**. It has a limit of an average of seven items (Miller, 1956). This capacity can be extended through 'chunking', e.g. 1,9,1,4;1,9,1,8,1,0,6,6 is easier to recall as three dates (1914, 1918 and 1066). The duration of STM has been investigated by Peterson and Peterson (1959) in a 'trigram retention experiment' and it was found to be approximately 18 seconds. The coding is mainly auditory (sound-based).
- **Long-term memory (LTM)**. It uses an abstract/semantic code (Baddeley 1966) and has a potentially unlimited capacity and indefinite duration.

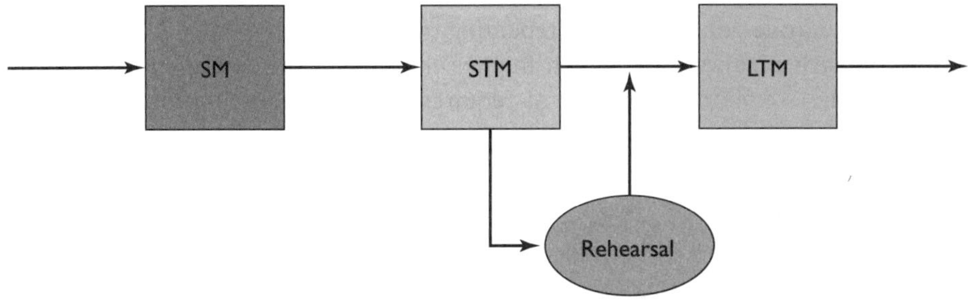

Figure 2 The multi-store model of memory

Study: Baddeley (1966)

Baddeley investigated coding in memory. Participants learned a list of acoustically similar words (tin, fin, win) and a list of semantically similar words (ill, sick, poorly). He found that more errors were made from the acoustically similar words on

Examiner tip
As part of your discussion of the theories of memory (multi-store, working memory, levels of processing) you should consider how the theories compare and contrast. This will help with your evaluation, e.g. a criticism of the multi-store model is that it oversimplifies the short-term memory whereas the working memory model addresses this by concentrating on short-term memory only.

Examiner tip
If you are outlining the multi-store model of memory, it is important to refer to both structure (short-term store and long-term store) and process (rehearsal).

Examiner tip
Make sure you know the properties of each store of the multi-store model, i.e. the duration, capacity and code.

Acoustic The sound (of the words).

Semantic The meaning (of the words).

immediate recall, but that more errors were made from the semantic condition when recall was delayed for 20 minutes. This was interpreted as STM using an acoustic code and LTM using a semantic code.

Evaluation

- Studies have shown that when participants are given a list of words to learn and are then allowed to recall them freely, they show superior recall from the beginning (primacy effect, words have reached LTM) and the end (recency effect, words are still in STM) of the list of words. (See the study by Murdock (1962) under 'Displacement theory of forgetting'.)
- Clinical studies of amnesiacs show that it is possible for STM to be damaged but LTM to remain intact, suggesting that the two stores must function separately.
- The model has been criticised for being oversimplified, with its view of a single short-term memory and a single long-term memory.
- Many of the studies supporting the model use laboratory experiments and therefore may tell us little about how memory works in real life.

Levels of processing theory (1972)

Craik and Lockhart (1972) proposed that **process** rather than **structure** is important to memory recall and that information can be processed at a number of different levels:

- shallow/structural level, e.g. what a stimulus looks like
- intermediate/phonetic level, e.g. the sound of the stimulus
- deep/semantic level — the meaning of the stimulus

Knowledge check 11

Distinguish between maintenance and elaborative rehearsal.

According to levels of processing theory, recall depends on how deeply information is processed rather than simply **rehearsal**.

Craik and Lockhart distinguished between two types of **rehearsal**:

(1) **maintenance rehearsal**, e.g. repeating the words
(2) **elaborative rehearsal**, which implies the processing of the meaning of the material — elaborative rehearsal requires deeper processing and results in a longer-lasting memory

Examiner tip

Be careful with the Craik and Tulving study. You must make it very clear that the *level of processing* was different in each condition. Students often make the error of saying participants recalled more of the semantic words than of the acoustic and visual words. This does not make any sense and does not get marks.

Study: Craik and Tulving (1975)

Craik and Tulving investigated levels of processing by giving participants a list of words and asking them to process each word at one of three levels: deep/semantic (assessing if a word fitted into a sentence), intermediate/acoustic (assessing the sound of a word) and shallow/structural (assessing whether a word was in capital or small letters). Recall was significantly higher when the words were processed at a deep level.

Evaluation

- One of the major problems with the levels of processing theory is that there is no adequate measure of processing depth and that circular reasoning is used: depth is usually defined as 'the number of words remembered', and the 'number of words remembered' is taken as a measure of depth.
- Another problem is that it is difficult to assess whether it is depth of processing or some other variable that improves recall. Studies have shown that processing effort, time spent processing, elaborative processing and distinctiveness all affect recall.
- The results of experiments testing levels of processing theory have generally supported predictions (e.g. Craik and Tulvings 1975).
- Craik (2002) has pointed out that the main contribution of the levels of processing theory was the emphasis on 'remembering as processing, as an activity of mind, as opposed to structural ideas of memory traces as entities that must be searched for'.

Examiner tip

The working memory model is a detailed model of short-term memory only.

The working memory model (WMM)

The term 'working' in the working memory model (Baddeley and Hitch 1974) emphasises how memory is involved in a range of everyday functions. The original model consisted of three components allowing for temporary storage of verbal and visuo-spatial material:

- The **phonological loop** stores verbal material and is concerned with auditory and speech-based information. This can be sub-divided into the **articulatory loop** (inner voice) and the **primary acoustic store** (inner ear).
- The **visuospatial scratchpad** or sketchpad (the inner eye) enables storage and processing of visual and spatial information.
- The **central executive** is an attentional system that coordinates and controls the other sub-components.

The original model of working memory has recently been revised and a fourth component, the **episodic buffer**, has been added (Baddeley 2000). The episodic buffer is a limited-capacity store that can access and assimilate information from a number of areas (e.g. visual and verbal) and allows the sub-systems to interact (see Figure 3).

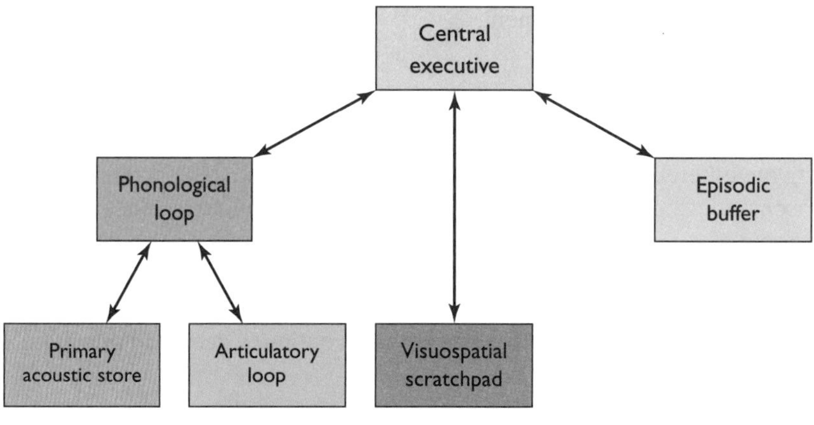

Figure 3 The working memory model

Concurrent At the same time.

Study: Farmer et al. (1986)

Farmer et al. asked participants to recite the digits: 1,2,3,4 (**articulatory suppression**) while performing either a spatial reasoning task or a verbal reasoning task. Concurrent performance of the verbal reasoning task was significantly disrupted, but articulatory suppression had no effect upon concurrent performance of the spatial reasoning task. In contrast, continuous sequential tapping (**spatial suppression**) produced significant interference only with spatial reasoning. These findings support Baddeley's proposal that the working memory has separate sub-systems: an articulatory loop and a visuo-spatial scratchpad.

Evaluation

- Evidence from several sources (e.g. experiments and case studies of brain-damaged patients) suggests that short-term memory does involve a number of interacting sub-components.
- Brain scans show that the verbal and spatial working memories are located in different areas of the brain.
- The central executive is considered to be the most important component of working memory; however, little is known about it.
- Evidence for working memory is largely based on laboratory experiments carried out in artificial environments, and it may be difficult to generalise findings from such studies to the way memory works in real life.

Examiner tip

Make sure you can distinguish between the three types of long-term store. Prepare an everyday example of each. Procedural memory often causes problems in exams; you must be clear that it is the memory for an action, like the memory for the action of swimming or throwing a ball.

Types of long-term memory

Tulving (1972) distinguished between different types of long-term store:

- **Episodic memory** — the memory of events, either personally experienced or about which we have read or heard. These memories are usually tied to a specific time and place.
- **Semantic memory** — this is the memory for general knowledge, a store of facts and information.
- **Procedural memory** — the memory of skills and actions, e.g. driving a car or playing a musical instrument.

Knowledge check 12

Give an example of an episodic memory.

Evaluation

- Brain imaging studies show that encoding and retrieval of episodic memories activate different areas of the brain from those activated in encoding and retrieval of semantic memories. This would suggest that there are indeed two different systems.
- Tulving (1984) has revised his original distinction between episodic and semantic memory and now proposes that they are part of the same system — they are not separate and independent. This has led to a continued debate in this area.

Explanations of forgetting

Summary specification content

Explanations of forgetting, including decay, interference, retrieval failure (absence of context and cues), displacement, lack of consolidation and motivated forgetting, including repression.

There are six theories of forgetting named on the specification. Some of these relate to short-term memory only (e.g. displacement), while the others relate to long-term memory (e.g. interference). You must know for each of these:

(1) the distinguishing features/components
(2) research evidence (studies)
(3) evaluation

Examiner tip
Displacement is an explanation of forgetting only in short-term memory and therefore should not be used if a question specifically asks for theories of forgetting in long-term memory.

Displacement theory of forgetting

According to the multi-store model of memory, short-term memory has a limited capacity of approximately seven items. When STM is full, any new items that enter the store 'push out' (displace) the older items from STM.

Evaluation

- Displacement appears to be an adequate explanation for forgetting in the short-term memory component of the multi-store model.
- This explanation of forgetting is too simplistic for the working memory model, which has a number of functionally different short-term stores.

Study: Murdock (1962)

Murdock gave participants a list of 20 common words at a rate of one word per second. After the last word, participants were asked to write down as many words from the list as they could remember. More words were recalled from the beginning of the list (the primacy effect) and the end of the list (the recency effect) than the middle of the list. One explanation for these findings, which supports the multi-store model of memory, is that the first items on the list were retrieved from LTM, whereas the items from the end of the list were still in STM. The items from the middle of the list had been displaced by the items at the end but had not yet reached LTM.

Decay theory of forgetting

When information enters short-term memory, it leaves a neural trace in the brain. This trace will spontaneously fade away unless it is strengthened, e.g. through rehearsal. According to Hebb (1949), if the trace is strengthened and becomes a permanent structural change (no longer a trace), this is long-term memory.

Evaluation

- According to this theory, if the trace has decayed, it has gone forever. However, some studies have shown that participants can recall information later on, even though it was not immediately available to them.
- Studies into the duration of STM have shown that after 30 seconds, when rehearsal is prevented, the trace completely decays, thereby supporting trace decay as a theory of forgetting.

Study: Peterson and Peterson (1959)

Peterson and Peterson presented participants with trigrams (e.g. JPX) that had to be held in STM for varying lengths of time (3 to 30 seconds). Rehearsal was prevented with a distracter task. They found a steady decline in recall, and after 30 seconds, no trigrams were recalled correctly. One way to interpret such findings is that, after this length of time, the trace has decayed, thereby supporting the trace decay theory of forgetting.

Knowledge check 13

Can you think of an alternative explanation for the findings in the Peterson and Peterson study?

Decay also explains forgetting from long-term memory. Ebbinghaus (1885) proposed that even well-established memories fade over time if they are not used.

Retrieval failure theory of forgetting

Retrieval failure theory suggests that information is not accessible because the appropriate retrieval cues are not being used. There are three types of retrieval cues:

(1) Context. Participants' recall is superior when they recall material in the same place in which they learned it.

(2) State. Performance on memory experiments is better when participants are in the same state (e.g. mood) when both learning and recall occur.

(3) Organisation. Participants recall more information if the material is organised (e.g. in a hierarchy) than if it is presented randomly (Bower 1969).

Knowledge check 14

How might retrieval failure affect your performance in an AS examination?

Study: Tulving (1968)

Tulving gave participants a list of words and then asked them to write down as many as they could remember immediately, and then on two further occasions. Tulving found that participants did not recall the same words each time and that words were sometimes recalled on the third occasion that had not been remembered earlier. If participants were using different cues on each occasion, retrieval failure can explain these findings (but trace decay cannot).

Evaluation

- The idea is appealing. We have all experienced the 'tip-of-the-tongue' phenomenon, where we know that we know something but cannot quite retrieve it.
- Studies carried out into **cue-dependent forgetting** have been criticised because they are often in extreme conditions (e.g. underwater) and therefore any findings may not generalise to everyday memory situations.

Cue-dependent forgetting To forget due to not having a signal or stimulus to prompt memory.

Interference theory of forgetting

Retroactive interference happens when recent learning interferes with the recall of earlier material. For example, you can remember your present telephone number but not your old one.

Proactive interference happens when earlier learning interferes with what you are trying to learn at present. For example, you know your old telephone number but cannot remember your new one.

Study: Keppel and Underwood (1962)

Keppel and Underwood asked participants to learn consonant trigrams (e.g. MXH) and then count backwards for varying lengths of time, from 3 to 18 seconds. On the first trial, regardless of whether participants counted for 3 seconds or 18 seconds, recall performance was 100%. However, on the second and third trials, recall performance fell as the interval increased. One explanation for these findings is that on later trials there was more interference from preceding items, i.e. proactive interference occurred.

Examiner tip

Students often confuse retroactive and proactive interference. 'Retro' means 'going back' and interfering with old material. 'Pro' means 'coming forward' and interfering with attempts to store new material.

Evaluation

- The effect of interference on memory is influenced by factors such as the similarity between the materials to be learned. Little interference is found on dissimilar material.
- Experiments to investigate interference may lack ecological validity; learning in a laboratory is unrealistically compressed in time and may not reflect either learning or recall in the real world.

Lack of consolidation as a theory of forgetting

A process of **consolidation** is required for information in short-term memory to become a long-term memory. Rehearsal causes neural activity and, in time, the activity leads to a structural change. These structural changes are 'solid' (consolidated) and equate to long-term memory. However, in the period of time that the consolidation is taking place, any physical or chemical disruption can cause memory loss as the active trace cannot become 'solid'. There is evidence that the consolidation period, when the memory is activated and reinforced, is up to 1 hour.

Study: Yarnell and Lynch (1970)

A field study was carried out on American footballers to investigate how head trauma can disrupt the consolidation process. Footballers who had been concussed during a game were asked about details of play at the time of the incident as soon as they 'came round', and then again 20 minutes later. When asked immediately, they gave accurate information. However, when asked 20 minutes later, this information was no longer available. It would appear that the blow to the head had disrupted the consolidation process and so the memory was never made permanent.

Knowledge check 15

What is a field study?

Spontaneous reactivation The reappearance of previously extinguished responses.

Evaluation

- Neuroscientists have recently found evidence for the **spontaneous reactivation** of learning in the brain of mice. If this process of activation is disrupted then memories cannot be consolidated.
- Evidence for consolidation theory comes from patients who have been concussed who often suffer a loss of memory for events just prior to the concussion. This may be because the consolidation process has been interrupted.

Motivated forgetting

Motivated forgetting Motivation is an internal state that drives us to action. In motivated forgetting we are not consciously aware of the drive to repress (and thereby not remember) an occurrence or thought.

Freud (1901) proposed that we are **motivated to forget** painful experiences that, if they were allowed to enter consciousness, would produce overwhelming anxiety. A traumatic event, such as witnessing a serious accident, may lead to **unconscious repression** of the memory. The memory is made inaccessible by this process of repression (which means that it is pushed below conscious awareness). Repression is an example of a Freudian defence mechanism, so called because it acts as a defence against something that would otherwise cause us anxiety. The repressed memories continue to affect behaviour even though we cannot recall them.

Knowledge check 16

How might repressed memories affect behaviour?

Study: Williams (1994)

Williams asked 100 women who had been sexually abused as children whether they remembered the incident 17 years later. Hospital records verified that the abuse had taken place. Thirty-eight per cent of the women reported no memory of the abuse. These results can be interpreted as offering support for the theory of 'repressive forgetting'. However, perhaps some of the women failed to report the abuse because of embarrassment, or because they did not want to discuss it at this stage in their lives.

Emotional inhibition Emotional terms such as 'sadness' and 'anger' are more difficult to recall than neutral terms.

Evaluation

- It is difficult to investigate motivated forgetting in the laboratory as participants would need to experience something anxiety-provoking, which would be unethical.
- Using mildly upsetting material, tests of **emotional inhibition** have offered some support for Freud's theory.
- It is usually the case that more pleasant memories are recalled than unpleasant memories, which motivated forgetting would predict. For example, we seem to forget unpleasant memories such as the pain of childbirth.
- However, we might recall pleasant memories better because we have rehearsed them more.

Summary

- The multi-store model of memory distinguishes between the structural components (STM and LTM), and memory processes (rehearsal and coding).
- The levels of processing theory proposed that process rather than structure is important to memory recall.
- The working memory model is a detailed model of short-term memory consisting of different components: phonological loop, visuospatial scratchpad, central executive.
- There are different types of long-term memory: episodic memory, semantic memory, procedural memory.
- Displacement theory of forgetting proposes that, when short-term memory is full, any new items that enter the store 'push out' (displace) older items.
- Decay theory of forgetting suggests that the neural trace in the brain spontaneously fades away unless it is strengthened, e.g. through rehearsal.
- Retrieval failure theory of forgetting suggests that information is not accessible because the appropriate retrieval cues are not being used.
- Interference theory of forgetting states that there are two types of interference: retroactive interference and proactive interference.
- Lack of consolidation theory states that physical disruption during the time needed for memories to become solid (consolidated) causes forgetting.
- Freud (1901) proposed a theory of motivated forgetting i.e. that we forget painful experiences via the process of unconscious repression.

Perceptual processes

Summary specification content

Perceptual set and the effects of motivation, expectation, emotion and culture on perception. Perceptual organisation. The Gestalt principles. Gibson's and Gregory's theories of visual perception. Depth cues, monocular and binocular. Types of perceptual constancy, including size constancy and shape constancy. Distortion illusions, including the Müller-Lyer illusion and the Ponzo illusion. Ambiguous figures, including the Necker cube and Rubin's vase. What distortion illusions and ambiguous figures tell us about perception.

Perceptual set

Perceptual set is an unconscious bias towards noticing some aspects of incoming data but not others. Vernon (1955) has suggested that set acts in two ways:

(1) as a **selector** — we focus our attention on what we expect to perceive
(2) as an **interpreter** — we already know how to interpret the incoming information and we are biased towards interpreting it this way

For example, when reading 'The dog chewed the bona', we might interpret 'bona' as 'bone' because our brain has automatically selected what to perceive in a given context.

Perceptual set and motivation

Studies seem to show that when we are deprived of something, our desire or motivation increases so we are more likely to perceive it. For example, if we are hungry, we may more readily smell food, or interpret the spoken words 'I scream' as something to eat (ice cream).

Knowledge check 17

Use an example to explain what psychologists mean by perceptual set.

Examiner tip

Four factors named on the specification are thought to influence perception and create a perceptual set — motivation, expectation, emotion and culture. You should be able to explain each factor and give a research example of each.

Study: Gilchrist and Nesberg (1952)

Gilchrist and Nesberg carried out an experiment with two groups of participants: one group was deprived of food, while the members of the other had eaten. All participants were then shown pictures and asked to rate them for brightness. Those who had been deprived of food rated the pictures of food and drink as visually brighter than the non-food pictures. The control group (who had eaten) showed no such difference in the ratings of food and non-food items.

Knowledge check 18

What was the purpose of the control group in the Gilchrist and Nesberg study?

Perceptual set and expectation

A number of studies have shown that we tend to perceive what we expect to see.

Study: Bruner and Minturn (1955)

Bruner and Minturn showed participants an ambiguous figure 'B' that could be interpreted as either the letter 'B' or the number '13'. Those shown the figure in the context of numbers — 12 B 14 — were more likely to interpret the figure as a '13', while those shown the figure in the context of letters — A B C — interpreted the figure as a letter. This shows how the interaction of context and expectation affects our perception.

Examiner tip

If asked in an examination question to discuss *at least two* factors affecting perceptual set, it is usually beneficial to discuss more than two. This is because for each factor you have the opportunity to outline the factor, discuss research evidence and comment evaluatively, thus gaining access to more marks.

Recognition threshold Point at which we can detect a stimulus.

Taboo Avoided, not usually spoken out loud in social situations.

Perceptual set and emotion

Our emotional state affects the way we perceive. Sometimes we are more likely to recognise something because of **perceptual sensitisation**. This is when the **recognition threshold** for a stimulus is lowered. At other times, our perceptual system defends us from upset or offence — this is known as **perceptual defence**. Perceptual defence means that we are less likely to perceive a stimulus. Things that cause us anxiety are more difficult to perceive at a conscious level.

Study: McGinnies (1949)

McGinnies investigated perceptual defence by presenting participants with emotionally neutral words (e.g. 'glass', 'apple') and '**taboo**' words (e.g. 'penis', 'rape'), and then asking them to name the word as soon as it was recognised. It was concluded that emotionally arousing taboo words led to perceptual defence.

Perceptual set and culture

Psychologists have been interested in discovering whether there are cultural differences in perception, i.e. whether the environment and culture in which a person lives affect the way that he or she perceives the world. Cross-cultural studies have indicated that there are cultural differences in the interpretation of visual illusions. For example, non-Europeans do not seem to interpret one line as being longer in the

Müller-Lyer illusion (see Figure 4). (The Müller-Lyer illusion is a visual illusion where two lines of equal length appear different because of the arrows pointing either inwards or outwards at both ends of each line.)

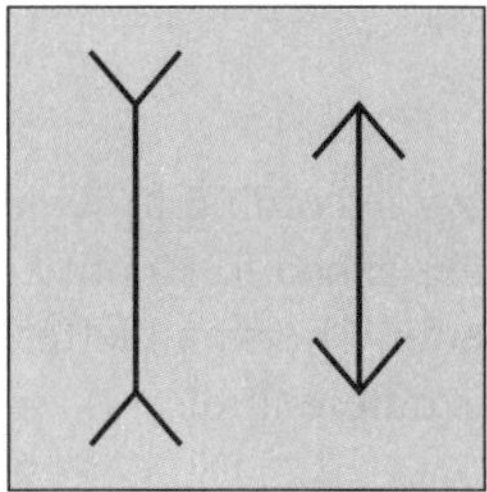

Figure 4 The Müller-Lyer illusion

Knowledge check 19

If perceiving perspective in drawings is learned, what would you expect to occur in young children's drawings?

Study: Deregowski (1972)

Deregowski investigated whether pictures were perceived in the same way in different cultures. Participants from African and European cultures were shown pictures that were either a split-type drawing or the same article showing perspective, and were asked to choose which they preferred. Africans preferred the split-type drawings, whereas Europeans chose the perspective drawings. Deregowski argued that perceiving perspective in drawings is a learned skill, and therefore culture must influence our perceptions.

Examiner tip

Knowledge of perceptual set supports Gregory's theory of visual perception. When you have studied theories of perception, think carefully about how perceptual set and Gregory's theory are linked.

Evaluation

- Depriving participants of food in studies can be criticised on ethical grounds. The use of 'taboo' words that may cause embarrassment and upset is also ethically unsound.
- Some of the studies have lacked ecological validity, for example the materials in the Gilchrist and Nesberg study were pictures, not real food items.
- One advantage is that the findings from studies into expectation can be used in the real world, for example in police training where personnel can be trained to notice and remember car registrations etc.
- Findings from cross-cultural studies can be interpreted in a culturally biased way by assuming, for example, that perspective drawings (favoured by Europeans) are artistically and culturally superior.

The Gestalt principles of perceptual organisation

Max Wertheimer was the founder of **Gestalt psychology**. He noticed that our visual system tended to organise material in predictable ways. He set out some 'laws of perceptual organisation', the underlying principle being the **Law of Pragnanz**. This law states that we attempt to perceive a coherent structure, and the visual system always perceives the simplest shape in an object. Gestalt psychologists assume that

Gestalt psychology A school of psychology founded in Germany in 1910.

'the whole is more than the sum of its parts'. In other words, when we perceive an object, we do not process individual elements but group things together to make a whole. Some of the main Gestalt laws of organisation are presented in the table below.

Study: Navon (1977)

Navon investigated the Gestalt law according to which 'the whole is more than the sum of its parts'. Participants were asked to identify either the small letters making up the large letter, or the large letter. The small letters were sometimes the same as the large letter (a) and sometimes different (b):

(a) L
L
L
LLLL

(b) X
X
X
XXXX

It took longer to identify the small letters when these conflicted with the shape of the large letter — in the example above, (b) would take longer than (a)— but there was no difference in the times taken to identify the large letters. This could be because the whole (large letter) was perceived before the parts (small letters), thus supporting the Gestalt rule.

Knowledge check 20

Name three Gestalt laws of organisation.

Law of organisation	Example
Similarity We tend to group together similar items. Here, we are likely to see rows in (a) but columns in (b).	**(a)** x x x x o o o o x x x x o o o o **(b)** o x o x o x o x o x o x o x o x
Proximity Items close together will tend to be grouped together. Here, we see three pairs of lines rather than six lines.	
Closure We tend to fill in (close up) missing information to make figures and characters whole. Here we can read 'old men rarely outlive old women'.	**Read this sentence** cld men rarely cutlive cld wcmen

Evaluation

- Some of the Gestalt laws seem to describe the perceptual organisation of two-dimensional items but cannot describe three-dimensional organisation.
- The Gestalt laws offer an adequate description of perceptual organisation but do not offer an explanation for the processes involved.
- The Gestalt laws have ecological validity as they can often explain real-life perception. For example, we tend to perceive a flock of birds as a group rather than as individual birds.

Depth cues: monocular and binocular

Depth perception allows us to view the world in three dimensions, even though our retinal image is two-dimensional. We determine the distance of objects by making use of two types of cue:

(1) cues from both eyes (**binocular**)
(2) cues from one eye only (**monocular**)

For objects far away from us, we rely mostly on monocular cues, but for closer objects we use both monocular and binocular cues.

Binocular depth cues

Convergence

Convergence is used for perceiving the distance of objects at close range. When the eyes converge on a near object (i.e. turn inwards as the object is brought closer), the angle between the eyes is greater than when they converge on a distant object. When looking at an object in the distance, the two eyes are parallel. It is from the stretching of the eye muscle that the brain can determine the distance of the object from us.

Examiner tip
You should be able to outline at least two monocular and two binocular depth cues.

Retinal disparity

Because the eyes are approximately 6 cm apart, there is a difference (disparity) between the images that fall on the retina at the back of each eye. The closer an object is to us, the greater this difference is. This disparity provides an important clue about the distance of objects.

Knowledge check 21
Name two binocular depth cues.

Monocular depth cues

Motion parallax

One monocular cue that involves movement and is therefore experienced in the natural environment is **motion parallax**. This is where movement of the head produces apparent movement of nearby objects in the opposite direction to us and distant objects in the same direction. In addition, when we are moving, objects close to us seem to pass by more quickly than objects in the distance. Because of the reasoning 'the faster an object passes by, the closer it must be', the visual system can estimate how far away any given object is.

Motion parallax This concerns the systematic movement in your visual field as you move about the environment.

Texture gradient

A coarser texture appears closer and a finer texture looks more distant, e.g. sand appears smooth in the distance but grainy close up.

Linear perspective

This refers to the tendency for parallel lines that recede from us to appear to converge.

Superposition or interposition

Objects that are closer to us partially obscure objects that are further away.

Examiner tip
Both size and shape constancies are named on the specification and therefore could be named in a question.

Constancy Perceiving objects as the same/similar even though the conditions of observation vary.

Knowledge check 22
Explain how perceptual constancies allow us to perceive birds in the sky as a normal size.

Illusion An illusion occurs when what we perceive cannot be predicted simply by analysing the physical stimulus.

Height in plane or elevation

When an object is further away, it appears higher in our visual field.

Perceptual constancies

Size constancy

When you move closer to an object, the size of the retinal image becomes larger but the perceived size of the object remains constant. This is because the brain receives information about both the size of the retinal image and the distance of the object, and the visual system automatically makes allowances for distance. This is size constancy.

Shape constancy

When we look at objects in real life, our viewpoints might be quite different and yet the perceived shape is the same. For example, when we see a door ajar, it makes a trapezium image on the retina, and yet we perceive it as a normal door. Two quite different viewpoints of the same object do not stop us from recognising it. This is shape constancy.

Distortion illusions and ambiguous figures

Distortion illusions

The two named illusions on the specification are:

- the Müller-Lyer illusion
- the Ponzo illusion

In the **Müller-Lyer illusion** (see Figure 4 on p. 31), the observer has to decide which of the two lines is longer. They are actually the same length, but the line with the outward arrows is usually perceived as longer. It has been found that people from Western cultures are more susceptible to this illusion. Segall et al. (1966) proposed that this illusion is cultural-specific because 'carpentered' cultures are used to seeing buildings that have angles resulting from intersections of ceilings and floors, and people automatically apply these learned depth cues to the arrows.

In the **Ponzo illusion** (see Figure 5), the top horizontal line appears longer than the line below it. These two lines must have the same retinal image since they are the same size. It is thought that false depth cues from the converging lines lead to the brain interpreting the top line as further away. If the line is further away, a smaller retinal image should be produced. However, this retinal image is of two lines of the same size, so the perceived size of the top line is expanded.

Figure 5 The Ponzo illusion

Ambiguous figures

The two named ambiguous figures on the specification are:

- the Necker cube
- Rubin's vase

With ambiguous figures, two hypotheses are presented to us and we are unable to make a definite interpretation of what our senses tell us.

The **Necker cube** is a line drawing of a cube that appears to change back and forth spontaneously between two distinct images — different orientations of the cube can be perceived. In Figure 6, the dot can be seen as inside the cube or outside it, depending on whether the cube is viewed as if from above or from below.

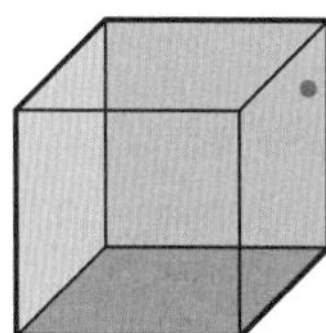

Figure 6 The Necker cube

In the **Rubin's vase** ambiguous figure, we can perceive either a green vase or two red faces. It is difficult to reject either figure because both are appropriate interpretations.

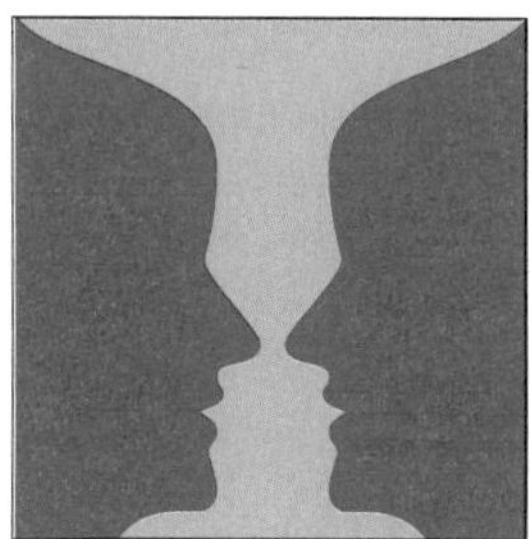

Figure 7 Rubin's vase

Examiner tip

Make sure you can describe the two distortion illusions and the two ambiguous figures named on the specification. It may be helpful to draw a diagram to help with the description.

What distortion illusions and ambiguous figures tell us about perception

By investigating the errors that are made in perception, psychologists have gained an insight into the automatic scaling mechanisms, such as size and shape constancy. They have been able to research visual perception in controlled laboratory environments to discover how perceptual processing occurs in the real world. For example, they have carefully manipulated the arrows in the Müller-Lyer illusion to investigate depth perception.

The study of ambiguous figures has shown the active nature of visual perception, offering support for Gregory's 'top-down' approach to perception (see next section). Research on ambiguous figures shows how perception can be manipulated by context and expectation. For example, if pictures of faces are shown prior to exposure to Rubin's vase, participants are much more likely to interpret the figure as faces than as the alternative vase figure. This shows how our perceptual hypotheses can be 'set', supporting the concept of 'perceptual set' and Gregory's theory of hypothesis testing.

Gibson's and Gregory's theories of visual perception

Gibson's theory of visual perception

Gibson argued that our perception of surfaces is important and that cues from the surfaces are given off and interpreted in a '**bottom-up**' fashion. This means that visual perception starts with sensory input from the object to the retina and finishes in the brain, where it is interpreted. Gibson thus proposed an **ecological theory** of perception whereby our perceptual system both perceives simple stimuli and decides what the object affords us (i.e. whether a surface can be sat on, slid on, grasped etc). He implied that not only the visual perception of an object, but also its *meaning*, are directly available. Gibson's theory is therefore a **direct theory** of perception. In addition to the concept of affordances, Gibson made two further fundamental points about the sensory input:

Affordances The intrinsic properties of an item, for example, a knife can be held, can cut, and so on.

- **Optic array**. In a natural environment, the light source from, say, a window gives off millions of rays of light. Some of these rays come directly from the object to the eye, and some come from the surface on which the object stands. Gibson proposed that the optic array from objects in our environment gives us a lot of helpful direct sensory data.
- **Invariants**. Textures expand as you approach an object and contract as you move away. This flow of texture always occurs in the same way and is, therefore, 'invariant'. This direct information from the environment provides an important cue to distance and depth.

Study: Lee and Lishman (1975)

A study was carried out by Lee and Lishman to investigate optic flow. They prepared a 'swaying room' where the floor moved and the texture flow could be manipulated. Participants were placed in the room to see if they could remain standing as the floor moved. Adults were able to make mental adjustments and they did not fall over. It was concluded that participants could monitor changes in the optic flow and send signals to their muscles.

Optic flow The changing sensory information that is given off from the environment with movement and received by the eyes.

Evaluation

- The experiment by Lee and Lishman lacked ecological validity because it would be rare to encounter a 'swaying room' in real life.
- One of the problems with Gibson's theory is that it cannot explain perceptual errors, e.g. visual illusions.
- Gibson's theory has ecological relevance and his work was stimulated by his interest in errors made by pilots in the Second World War.
- The concept of invariants has led to interesting empirical research, for example into the perception of ageing faces.

Gregory's theory of visual perception

Gregory (1972) proposed a constructivist **approach** to perception that relies on '**top-down**' processing. This means that expectations stored in the brain work downwards to influence the way we interpret the sensory information from a stimulus. In visual perception, sensory receptors in the retina trigger neural activity, and knowledge in the brain interacts with inputs from the stimulus to enable us to make sense of the world around us. One type of evidence for Gregory's theory lies in the way we perceive what we expect to see in a particular context, thereby drawing on stored knowledge. For example, read the following sentence:

'Hush-a-bye baby on a tree top; when the wind bows, the cradle will rock.'

You probably read 'blows' instead of 'bows', because that is what you would expect to find in this sentence.

Evidence for Gregory's active approach to perception can be found in his explanation of the Müller-Lyer illusion (see Figure 4 on p. 31). He proposed that the arrows at the ends of the lines provide cues to depth. The outgoing arrows suggest the inside corner of a room, and the ingoing ones resemble the outside corner of a building. In the real world, these inward- and outward-facing corners are cues to distance. Gregory's **misapplied size constancy theory** states that the outgoing arrows are giving off depth cues that suggest that this line is further away. The retinal image is of two lines that are equal in length. If this is so, then the one that is assumed to be further away must be longer. As a result, our perception of this line is mentally 'scaled up'.

Constructivist
Perceptual experience is more than a direct response to stimulation but includes hypotheses based on (constructed from) past experiences.

Evaluation

- When the arrows are removed from the Müller-Lyer illusion and replaced by circles, there are no depth cues. The illusion, however, persists and this is a problem for the 'misapplied size constancy theory' proposed by Gregory.
- A lot of the research carried out by Gregory is in a laboratory situation using visual illusions. This lacks ecological validity because in the real world, as Gibson points out, there are a lot of rich sensory data to aid perception.
- Unlike Gibson, Gregory can explain visual illusions.
- It is likely that both bottom-up (Gibson) and top-down (Gregory) approaches are used in perception, depending on the environmental conditions.

Knowledge check 23

Identify and outline two points of comparison between Gregory and Gibson.

Summary

- 'Perceptual set' is an unconscious bias towards noticing some aspects of incoming data but not others.
- There are four factors that influence perceptual set: motivation, expectation, emotion and culture.
- Gestalt psychologists assume that 'the whole is more than the sum of its parts', and they have proposed the Gestalt laws of organisation.
- Depth perception allows us to view the world in three dimensions, even though our retinal image is two-dimensional. We determine the distance of objects by making use of two types of cue: binocular and monocular.
- Size and shape constancies allow us to perceive the world in a consistent way.

Summary

- Illusion occurs when what we perceive cannot be predicted simply by analysing the physical stimulus, as illustrated in the Müller-Lyer and the Ponzo illusions.
- Ambiguous figures present us with two hypotheses that we have difficulty interpreting, for example, the Necker cube and Rubin's vase.
- Gibson's direct theory of perception argued that cues from surfaces in the environment are interpreted in a 'bottom-up' fashion.
- Gregory's constructivist approach to perception relies on 'top-down' processing.

Individual differences

Anxiety disorders

Phobias and obsessive-compulsive disorder

Summary specification content

Phobias: definition and symptoms. Agoraphobia, social phobias and specific phobias.

Explanations of phobias, including behavioural and psychodynamic. Treatments for phobias, including systematic desensitisation and psychodynamic therapy. Evaluation of these treatments.

Obsessive-compulsive disorder: definition and symptoms. The difference between obsession and compulsion. Explanations of obsessive-compulsive disorder, including biological and cognitive. Treatments for obsessive-compulsive disorder, including drug therapy and cognitive therapy. Evaluation of these treatments.

Phobias

Phobias are extreme fears of an object, organism or situation (or several). These fears are disproportionate to the danger actually posed, and this usually leads to the object of the fear being avoided. A fear becomes a phobia when it becomes **maladaptive**, that is, when it interferes with everyday life.

Knowledge check 24

(i) Give two symptoms of phobias. (ii) Identify three types of phobia and give an example of each.

Maladaptive Not adaptive, i.e. not able to function normally.

Examiner tip

If asked to define a phobia, do make sure you state that it is an *extreme* and disproportionate fear — not simply a fear.

Different types of phobias

Specific phobia

Someone with a specific phobia avoids a particular object (e.g. needles), organism (e.g. spiders) or situation (e.g. heights) because of the intense and irrational fear caused. If he or she is faced with the specific object or situation, anxiety and panic will occur. Even thinking about it can cause panic. To be diagnosed as suffering from a specific phobia, the fear must be excessive, be triggered immediately on exposure and interfere with everyday functioning.

Social phobia

A social phobia is an excessive and irrational fear of one or more social situations, particularly of being scrutinised and humiliated in public. There are two types of social phobia:

(1) Generalised social phobia. This is a fear of a variety of social interactions, such as speaking to people, going to parties etc.

(2) Social phobia for specific situations (e.g. public speaking). Panic will arise if the individual is faced with such a social situation, so these are avoided wherever possible.

When the social anxiety begins to interfere with everyday life, a phobia may be diagnosed.

Agoraphobia

This is the most serious phobic disorder. It is associated with a fear of leaving home, being in a crowd, visiting public places, travelling on buses, planes etc., or a fear of having a panic attack in a public place and being unable to find help. It can lead to the sufferer becoming housebound.

Explanations of phobias

Behavioural explanation

Behaviourists propose a two-process theory for the acquisition of phobias because it involves both classical and operant conditioning. A person can learn to fear a previously neutral stimulus if it is associated with a frightening stimulus. For example, if each time you see a spider someone screams, a learned association between the two stimuli will develop. Eventually, through simple association, the fear response will be produced to the spider (even with no scream). This response of fear is then maintained by operant conditioning because when the stimulus is avoided the fear is reduced, and this is rewarding. For example, contact with spiders is avoided in order to avoid the fearful response. This is sometimes called **avoidance conditioning**.

Study: Watson and Rayner (1920)

Watson and Rayner investigated the classical conditioning of a phobia with Albert, who at 9 months had no fear of rats. At 11 months old, Albert was presented with a white rat and when he touched it a loud bang was made behind him. The rat and loud bang were presented over a period of 7 days, and Albert showed distress. After a while, the rat on its own, without the loud bang, elicited distress — Albert had been 'conditioned' to fear the animal.

Evaluation

- People tend to be fearful of certain objects or organisms (e.g. needles, spiders, snakes) but not of others (e.g. ladybirds). It might be that we are physiologically prepared to be readily classically conditioned to fear some objects more than we fear others.

Examiner tip

There are two named explanations of phobias on the specification (behavioural and psychodynamic). You should be able to describe, evaluate and refer to evidence for each explanation.

Classical conditioning
A form of associative learning whereby a conditioned stimulus (CS) that does not elicit a particular response is paired a number of times with an unconditioned stimulus (UCS) that normally does elicit the particular response, resulting in the CS alone producing the response. This was investigated by Pavlov.

Operant conditioning
A form of associative learning whereby responses to stimuli are encouraged/strengthened by reinforcement. This was investigated by Skinner.

Knowledge check 25

What was the unconditioned stimulus in the Watson and Rayner study?

Evaluation

- Although it can be demonstrated that fears can be acquired through classical conditioning (e.g. Little Albert), this does not mean that in the real world all fears are acquired this way. Fears that develop gradually, e.g. social phobias, cannot be adequately explained by this approach.

Psychodynamic explanation

According to Freud, phobias are a way of dealing with the anxiety produced by repressed id impulses. If an id impulse has been punished in childhood, this impulse will no longer be openly expressed. An example that Freud used is the young boy's attraction to his mother (an unconscious id impulse) and fear of castration by his father. This **id impulse** is managed by the ego, the rational part of personality, and is repressed into the unconscious but still causes anxiety. This anxiety is displaced (moved) to another object that often has symbolic connections to the original object. Thus, Little Hans becomes fearful of horses with blinkers because they remind him of his father (see study below). By avoiding horses, the boy can avoid dealing with his repressed childhood fear of castration.

Id impulse The primitive, unconscious element of Freud's tripartite personality structure that is governed by the pleasure principle, and demands instant gratification.

Study: Freud (1909)

Freud conducted a case study to investigate a young boy's phobia of horses. He proposed that the boy, Hans, had developed the phobia due to an unresolved **Oedipal conflict** in childhood. According to Freud, Hans desired his mother and feared his father because the father was big and strong. Hans particularly feared castration and had **displaced** this fear of his father onto horses and developed a phobia.

Displacement A Freudian defence mechanism whereby emotions are transferred from the original object/person to a different object/person.

Evaluation

- The evidence for the psychodynamic explanation of phobias is derived from case studies and therefore is subjective.
- There is a simpler behavioural explanation for the acquisition of Hans's phobia: at the age of 4, he had witnessed an accident in the street when a horse had collapsed. This could have caused a classically conditioned fear of horses.

Knowledge check 26

Briefly explain why case studies are considered subjective.

Treatments of phobias

Systematic desensitisation

This treatment replaces anxiety with relaxation and is generally achieved by following a number of steps:

(1) The patient learns how to relax.
(2) A hierarchy of anxiety is constructed whereby the patient ranks situations, from the least to the most anxiety-provoking.

(3) The exposure stage, where the patient starts with the least anxiety-provoking situation and learns to relax while engaging with the phobic object, for example, looking at a picture of a spider while remaining in a relaxed state. Then the patient moves to the next stage, for example, remaining relaxed while looking at a real spider in a cage. The patient moves up the hierarchy until he or she can remain relaxed in the most anxiety-provoking situation, for example, holding a spider.

This treatment can also be carried out using imagery instead of actual fearful situations. More recently, virtual reality exposure therapy (VRET) has been introduced, where patients are placed in a three-dimensional virtual world.

Examiner tip

An essential part of systematic desensitisation is the relaxation, as the treatment is based on the assumption that two competing emotions (fear and relaxation) cannot occur together (this is desensitisation). It is important that you refer to this if asked to outline the technique in the examination, as well as the graded exposure (which is the systematic part of the procedure).

Evaluation

- Systematic desensitisation is particularly effective for specific phobias (e.g. of snakes). Lang and Lazovik (1963) found improvement for snake phobia both immediately and six months after treatment, compared to a control group.
- Richards (2002) found systematic desensitisation 'in vivo' (real-life, not imagery) is the most effective technique.

Psychodynamic therapy

In order for patients to deal with their anxiety disorder, they have to confront their fears, and the **ego defence mechanisms** that are in place to protect them from anxiety have to be lifted. **Insight** can then be gained into what is unconsciously causing the symptoms. Various techniques can be used to access the unconscious, including free association. This is where the patient relaxes and says out loud everything that comes into his or her mind. As he or she relaxes, the ego has difficulty managing the unconscious id impulses, which begin to slip through. These can then be interpreted by the analyst.

Ego defence mechanisms Processes that help the ego to manage the energies arising from the id impulses.

Insight Occurs when we begin to understand the inner nature of something.

Evaluation

- There are much quicker and more effective ways of dealing with anxiety, for example, systematic desensitisation.
- The analysis of the unconscious can prove traumatic for patients as, when the defence mechanisms are lifted, negative emotions such as guilt and fear are released.

Obsessive-compulsive disorder (OCD)

Obsessions are automatic, disturbing, recurring thoughts and images that intrude into one's mind. **Compulsions** are behaviours that an individual feels compelled to perform in order to reduce the anxiety caused by obsessive thoughts.

Examiner tip

When defining obsessions and compulsions, take care — 'obsessions' are not just thoughts and 'compulsions' are not simply behaviours.

Explanations of obsessive-compulsive disorder

Biological explanations

- **Genetic factors**. Family studies have indicated that there is a predisposition to the illness. Pauls et al. (1995) found that 10% of patients with OCD had relatives who suffered from OCD, compared to 1.9% in a control group with no OCD relatives.
- **Biochemical factors**. OCD seems to be related to low levels of the neurotransmitter serotonin. Drugs such as selective serotonin reuptake inhibitors (SSRIs) (antidepressants) increase the levels of serotonin and at the same time appear to reduce OCD symptoms.

Examiner tip

Make sure you get the serotonin levels the right way round, i.e. *low* serotonin levels are linked to the cause of anxiety and SSRIs *increase* serotonin levels.

Evaluation

- It is difficult to untangle genetic and environmental influences. It might be that close relatives of OCD sufferers observe and imitate the behaviour.
- The fact that SSRIs have a therapeutic effect does not necessarily imply that low levels of serotonin *cause* OCD.

Knowledge check 27

Briefly explain how genetic and environmental influences on OCD could be investigated using identical twins.

Cognitive explanation

People who suffer from OCD have obsessive thoughts that cause great anxiety. They have a **cognitive bias** that can make them '**hypervigilant**' when attending to environmental stimuli. This makes them more likely to attend to threat-related stimuli. Unlike most people, OCD sufferers seem unable to banish unwanted thoughts, and the thoughts and images become ever more vivid and intolerable.

It has also been found that OCD sufferers can have a number of memory deficits. For example, they really cannot remember if the door is locked, even after checking, and they have little confidence in their own memory ability.

Examiner tip

Students often find cognitive explanations quite difficult. In an answer, make sure you refer to terms such as 'cognitive bias' and 'hypervigilance'.

Cognitive bias Inclined to think about, pay attention to and perceive things in the environment in a particular way; for example, a person with obsessive thoughts of contamination may pay more attention to cutlery in a restaurant.

Hypervigilant Excessively watchful.

Evaluation

- The cognitive approach focuses on the internal cognitions that account for OCD, but cannot explain social and emotional aspects of the condition.
- Treatment aimed at reducing hypervigilance in OCD sufferers has had some success, suggesting that this may be a contributory factor.

Treatments of obsessive-compulsive disorder (OCD)

Drug therapy

Antidepressants are the main medications prescribed for OCD. These include Prozac, which is an SSRI (it increases the level of the neurotransmitter serotonin in the brain). This drug has proved particularly effective for OCD, as this anxiety disorder is frequently accompanied by depression.

Evaluation

- All drugs have some side effects, and those of SSRIs include sickness and headaches. It also takes a number of weeks for SSRIs to begin to have an effect. This, together with the side effects that have to be endured, leads some people to stop taking the medication.
- When drug therapy stops, the patient relapses and a combined drug therapy and psychological treatment is therefore preferred for long-term benefits.

Counterproductive thought A thought that is not productive/helpful.

Counterstatement A statement that goes against a thought and challenges it.

Knowledge check 28

Give one counter-productive thought and one counterstatement that a therapist could use with an obsessive checker of locked windows/doors.

Cognitive therapy

Cognitive therapy aims to replace fearful thoughts (obsessions) with more realistic ones. It teaches patients to challenge **counterproductive thoughts** with counterstatements. For example, the catastrophic thought 'If I do not wash my hands after touching a door handle, I will die of contamination' can be challenged, and a **counterstatement** might be: 'No one I know has died from touching a door handle. It is very unlikely to happen.' Often cognitive treatment is combined with behaviour therapy, for example Beck's cognitive behaviour therapy, which applies behaviourist principles such as systematic desensitisation but also attempts to alter irrational thought processes.

Examiner tip

Students often confuse the two anxiety disorders (phobias and OCD). Look carefully at the wording on the question in the examination and consider: Is the question about phobias or OCD? Is the question concerning explanations or treatments? If the question is on explanations and you refer to treatments, you must do so in an evaluative way to gain marks.

Evaluation

- Cognitive therapy combined with behaviour therapy has proved remarkably effective in the treatment of OCD.
- It is not clear what part of the cognitive therapy is effective in changing cognitions and it could be that any cognitive change is a consequence of some other factor, such as exercise, and not the cognitive therapy.

Summary

- Anxiety disorders include phobias and obsessive-compulsive disorder.
- Phobias are extreme fears of an object, organism or situation, which are disproportionate to the danger actually posed.
- The three named types of phobia are specific, social, agoraphobia.
- Behaviourists propose a two-process theory for the acquisition of phobias because it involves both classical and operant conditioning.
- A behavioural treatment for phobias is systematic desensitisation, where a patient starts with the least anxiety-provoking situation and learns to relax while engaging with the phobic object.
- Psychodynamic theory proposes that phobias are a way of dealing with the anxiety produced by repressed id impulses.
- Psychodynamic therapy includes free association.
- In obsessive-compulsive disorder (OCD) the obsessions are automatic, disturbing, recurring thoughts and images whereas the compulsions are behaviours that an individual feels compelled to perform in order to reduce anxiety.
- Biological explanations for OCD include genetics and biochemistry.
- Drug therapy for OCD usually involves the use of antidepressants.
- Cognitive explanations propose that people who suffer from OCD have obsessive thoughts that cause great anxiety. They have a cognitive bias that can make them 'hypervigilant' when attending to environmental stimuli.
- Cognitive therapy aims to replace fearful thoughts (obsessions) with more realistic ones.

Autism

Definition, symptoms, treatments, explanations and studies of autism

Summary specification content

Definition and symptoms, including lack of joint attention. Autism as a syndrome: the triad of impairments. Biological explanations, including genetics and neurological correlates. Cognitive explanations, including theory of mind, central coherence deficit and failure of executive functioning. Studying autism: the Sally-Anne experiment, the 'Smarties tube' test, comic-strip stories. Therapeutic programmes for autism, including drug therapy, behaviour modification (including the Lovaas technique), parental involvement. Evaluation of these programmes.

Prevalence The total number of cases (e.g. 8) in a specified population (e.g.10,000) at a point in time.

Definition and symptoms of autism

Autism is a developmental disorder that starts early in childhood, with a **prevalence** rate of approximately 8 per 10,000, and it is four times more likely to be diagnosed in boys than girls. The features first identified by Kanner (1943) are still used in diagnosis today. For diagnosis to be made, impairment in three areas is necessary, with at least six of the behaviours noted:

- **Social interaction**. Poor use of eye gaze and gestures; lack of personal relationships, sharing and social/emotional reciprocity.
- **Communication**. Delay in the acquisition of language/speech; repetitive and stereotyped language; failure to initiate/sustain conversation; lack of play.
- **Restricted activities**. Repetitive or stereotyped movements; narrow/intense interests; strict adherence to routines and rituals.

Knowledge check 29

Outline two symptoms of autism.

Examiner tip

The term 'joint attention' occurs on the specification so make sure you know what this means and can give an example. Also, note that joint attention seems to be a normal developmental occurrence that autistic children *do not* show.

Autistic children seem to have a particular deficit in what is called '**joint attention**': a child aged around 12 months will attempt to interact socially with an adult by engaging his or her attention on to a shared object. The child might look at the adult and then look at a toy, maybe pointing, in such a way that the adult's attention is drawn to the same toy and then back to the child. This is an early preverbal activity that autistic children do not seem to develop.

Triad of impairments Impairments in three areas.

When a set of symptoms occur together and have a common origin, they are known as a **syndrome**. There seems to be a **triad of impairments** (poor social interaction, poor communication, repetitive and stereotyped behaviour) that regularly occur together in autism, and some researchers believe that this can be considered a syndrome.

Knowledge check 30

Explain why autism is sometimes referred to as a 'syndrome'.

Explanations of autism

Biological explanations

Genetics

Concordance Agreement: that is, the extent to which, if one person is diagnosed with autism, so is another.

Concordance studies have shown that if one child in a family has autism, there is a 3–6% chance of a sibling being diagnosed with it, which is much higher than the risk of autism in the normal population. Research into monozygotic (MZ) twins (who have identical genetic make-up) provides the strongest support for a genetic component, with consistently higher concordance rates found for MZ twins than for dizygotic (DZ) twins, siblings or other relatives.

Study: Ritvo et al. (1985)

Ritvo et al. investigated the genetic component of autism in MZ and DZ twins. They found concordance rates for 23 MZ twin pairs to be 96%, while only 23% for 17 DZ twin pairs. This provides strong evidence that autism is inherited.

Evaluation

- Although family and twin studies point to genetic factors being a likely cause of autism, the mode of genetic transmission is still being investigated.
- The number of twin pairs available to study is low because both twins and autism are relatively rare.
- It is likely that there is a genetic predisposition for autism, but environment must play some part too: although DZ twins and siblings have the same proportion of genetic similarity (50%), the DZ concordance rates for autism are widely different — 23% and 2% respectively.

Knowledge check 31

Explain why the rarity of the twin population is considered a problem when using twin concordance data to study autism.

Neurological correlates

Research into structural abnormalities of the autistic brain has been carried out post-mortem (after death). A number of abnormal areas have been identified this way, including the frontal lobes, the limbic system and the brain stem and cerebellum. Recent advances in neuroimaging have led to greater insight into the autistic brain in children because researchers have been able to examine the live brain. Two techniques used are single photon emission computed tomography (**SPECT**) and magnetic resonance imaging (**MRI**).

Study: Ohnishi et al. (2000)

Using SPECT, Ohnishi et al. found unusually high blood flow in a number of brain regions of a group of autistic children. For example, they found a strong positive correlation between high blood flow in the frontal cortex and deficits in communication and social interaction.

Unlike SPECT, MRI does not require radiation and therefore is the preferred method for use with children. A number of studies using MRI have found the cerebellum and brain stem to be significantly smaller in autistic individuals.

Examiner tip

The key assumption underlying these correlational studies, which show brain differences between a 'normal' and an 'autistic' brain, is that autism is a result of the identified brain differences. This would be important to point out in a discussion, as it contains a causal flaw — an unwarranted assumption of a causal relationship.

Study: Piven et al. (1995)

Piven et al. used MRI and found an excessive enlargement of the brain in autistic individuals compared to normal individuals and people with learning difficulties.

Evaluation

- Variables such as age, gender and IQ differ between autistic samples and controls in neuroimaging studies, which makes comparison difficult.
- Although regions of the brain responsible for some autistic symptoms have been identified, there are still many other symptoms not accounted for by brain differences.
- Brain differences may be a result of the disorder rather than the cause.

Cognitive explanations

Theory of mind

Theory of mind The understanding that other people can be perceiving the world in a different way from you.

Autistic children do not seem to think about mental states in the same way as normal children do. Research has shown that at about 4 years old, normal children begin to attribute mental states to others, but in autistic children this ability fails to develop. Studies have investigated the failure of autistic children to develop a **theory of mind** — an understanding of how the mind works. Baron-Cohen et al. (1985) came to the conclusion that autistic children are 'mind-blind'. This 'mind-blindness' might explain some of the social, emotional and communication problems found in autistic people.

Autistic savants A small proportion of autistic individuals are known as 'savants', in that they have an extraordinary ability in a particular area such as mathematics.

Evaluation

- It is not clear whether lacking a theory of mind is a cause or a symptom of autism.
- Lack of theory of mind accounts for some of the symptoms of autism, such as social and communication impairments, but cannot explain other symptoms such as islets of ability shown by **autistic savants**.

Examiner tip

The Sally–Anne experiment outlined on p. 47 is useful evidence for the apparent lack of a theory of mind in autistic individuals.

Central coherence deficit

Humans tend to process information for general meaning rather than focusing on individual elements. For example, when we listen to the weather forecast, we remember the gist of the message rather than each individual word. According to Frith (1989), autistic individuals are not able to process stimuli in a general way. Instead of focusing on the 'whole', they attend to individual elements. This might account for both the deficits and the enhanced abilities found in some cases of autism.

Study: Shah and Frith (1993)

Shah and Frith gave a group of autistic and non-autistic children the 'Children's Embedded Figures Test', where a small figure has to be located in the midst of other shapes. Autistic children were significantly faster at this task. One explanation for this is that they do not succumb to the normal cognitive process of perceiving the 'whole' — they have weak central coherence.

Evaluation

- Weak central coherence is only one explanation for the advantage that autistic individuals seem to have on tasks such as the embedded figures test. Other theories, such as superior low-level processing, can also account for these findings.
- A small proportion of autistic individuals are known as 'savants', i.e. they have an extraordinary ability in a particular area. Such individuals show great attention to detail, and weak central coherence can explain some of their exceptional abilities.

Failure of executive functioning

When we attempt to override automatic behaviour, initiate change in our behaviour or multi-task we are engaging in 'higher-order' functions, sometimes called **executive functions**. Autistic individuals have particular difficulty with these types of processes as they spend much of their time on routine and repetitive behaviour and find change hard to cope with. Impaired executive functioning has been proposed as a theory to explain these specific higher-order cognitive deficits associated with autism. Neuroimaging studies have found evidence for frontal-lobe abnormality in autistic individuals, and this area is also at least partly responsible for higher-level cognitive functions.

Examiner tip

Note that all three cognitive theories propose a deficit in a particular area: i.e. autistic children do not develop a theory of mind; they have weak central coherence; and they have impaired executive functioning.

Evaluation

- The symptoms associated with autism are so wide-ranging that it is unlikely one cognitive theory can account for them all. The impaired executive functioning explanation complements the theory of mind explanation, accounting for additional problems associated with autism.
- The evidence from neuroimaging studies supports cognitive theories. It is possible that failure of executive function originates in a malfunction of the frontal lobe area of the brain.

Studying autism

Studies have shown that children with autism have a particular difficulty understanding another person's **false belief**.

False belief An understanding that another person may not know what you know.

The Sally–Anne experiment

Baron-Cohen et al. (1985) tested three groups of children: a group of autistic children aged 6–16 years; a group with Down's syndrome of similar age but with a verbal ability of 3 years; a control group of 'normal' children aged 4 years. Children were individually introduced to two dolls: Sally carrying a basket and Anne with a box. Sally placed a marble in her basket and went for a walk. Anne transferred the marble to the box. Sally returned and the child was asked, 'Where will Sally look for her marble?' Only 20% of autistic children could answer the question correctly, whereas over 80% of 'normal' and Down's syndrome children answered correctly. It was concluded that autistic children lack a 'theory of mind'.

The 'Smarties tube' test

Perner et al. (1989) showed children ('normal' and autistic) a Smarties tube and asked 'What do you think is in this tube?' They answered 'Smarties' but were then shown that it actually contained a pencil. The pencil was put back into the tube and they were asked what their friend would think was in the tube. Three-year-old normal children answered 'A pencil', but 4-year-olds answered correctly 'Smarties'. Two-thirds of the autistic group answered 'A pencil' and could not understand that other people would have a false belief and think that there were Smarties in the tube. It was concluded that autistic children do not seem to understand others' false beliefs.

Knowledge check 32

At what age does the 'Smarties tube' study suggest that an understanding of false belief develops in 'normal' children?

Comic-strip stories

Baron-Cohen et al. (1986) used a set of four pictures that made up either a mechanical story (no people involved), a behavioural story (which included people, but no understanding of their thinking was required) and a mentalistic story (which required an understanding of the beliefs of the people in the pictures). The four pictures in each strip were mixed up and the children were required to place them in the correct order while explaining the story. Autistic children could do the mechanical and behavioural tasks but not the mentalistic one. The mentalistic task required an understanding of the minds of the characters, which autistic children did not seem to have.

Evaluation

- The failure of autistic children at these tasks might explain their social deficits. However, it tells us nothing about other symptoms such as repetitive behaviour or the specific abilities that some autistic individuals possess.
- Some researchers have suggested that the cognitive demands were too great, e.g. the autistic children may have had difficulty with the wording of the questions.

Therapeutic programmes for autism

Drug therapy

Medication can be used to treat the symptoms of autism. Common drug treatments used with autistic children include:

- Haloperidol and Risperidone. These are antipsychotic drugs that can reduce social withdrawal, stereotyped motor behaviour and self-abusive behaviours.
- Fluoxetine (Prozac) and similar antidepressants influence the serotonin levels and are used to treat high-functioning people with autism.
- A study by McCracken et al. (2002) looked at the effectiveness of Risperidone in controlling symptoms such as tantrums and aggression in autistic young people. A significant reduction in irritability was noted both immediately and at six-month follow-up, although side effects such as drowsiness and drooling were significantly higher in the drug group than the **placebo group**.

Examiner tip
Note that all the treatments outlined here are named on the specification and you should be able to discuss them all.

Placebo group A control group given 'medication' with no active ingredients.

Evaluation

- Drugs are not a cure and are given to control the symptoms of autism; the side effects of the drugs can be problematic.
- The drugs can improve the quality of life for both autistic individuals and their carers.

Behaviour modification

Behaviour is changed through a process of shaping where small pieces of required behaviour are positively reinforced. **Applied behavioural analysis (ABA)** uses reinforcement and behaviour shaping to improve linguistic skills and specific behaviours, and has proved effective. **Discrete trial training (DTT)** is an individual training programme introduced by Lovaas (1987) whereby behaviour is broken down into discrete components and each component is positively reinforced. There are three parts to the programme:

- **Antecedent**. An individual is given a request, such as 'Choose a plate, Amy'.
- **Behaviour**. The adult waits for a response (e.g. Amy responds by choosing a plate). (Note that there is an element of choice purposely as this has been found to improve the outcome.)
- **Consequence**. The adult responds, 'Well done Amy, good choice, now choose something to eat'.

Study: Lovaas (1989)

Lovaas investigated the effectiveness of ABA by giving 19 autistic children under the age of 4 intensive behaviour therapy for 40 hours a week for 2 years. There was a control group who received no therapy. After the 2 years, most children were able to join mainstream school and 47% of the treatment group had a normal IQ level, with a further 40% at the mildly retarded IQ level. This compared to 2% and 45% respectively for the control group. Those in the treatment group who returned home continued to improve.

Knowledge check 33

Briefly explain the purpose of the control group in the Lovaas study.

Evaluation

- Behaviour modification has proved to be one of the most effective long-term treatments for children with autism.
- There have been a number of methodological criticisms of the Lovaas study, such as no random assignment to groups. Other studies have shown that if the skill of the child was poor before treatment, no amount of intensive training would benefit him or her.

Language training

Lovaas et al. (1967) used **behaviour shaping** to train autistic children to communicate more effectively. The required behaviour would be first broken down into constituent parts, for example (a) making eye contact, (b) making a sound, (c) making a relevant consonant sound etc., and successive approximations towards the word are then rewarded, usually with food as a **positive reinforcer**. This type of language training has become known as the 'Lovaas technique'. Although extremely time-consuming, it has been successful.

Positive reinforcer A reward that increases the probability of the behaviour being repeated.

Computers have recently been introduced to teach language and communication skills to children with autism. Bosseler and Massaro (2003) developed a computer tutor to teach vocabulary and grammar. Their computer-animated programme included **receptive language** and **expressive language** activities, and was successful both during the study and when the children returned to their natural environment.

Receptive language Concerned with language comprehension.

Expressive language Concerned with vocal language.

Parental involvement

Improvement is greater and better maintained when parents/caregivers are involved in a therapeutic programme. Involving parents can help in the generalisation of behaviours acquired in a therapeutic situation to a range of different everyday contexts. Parents are present at crucial times through the day and can reinforce appropriate

Knowledge check 34

Briefly explain why it is important to involve parents/caregivers in a therapeutic programme.

behaviours immediately as and when they occur. They can also withhold reinforcers for inappropriate behaviour. Where parents are committed to the programme, results are encouraging.

Evaluation

- Lovaas found that the involvement of parents was a key element in the success of his therapy. He found that children who were sent back to institutions quickly regressed, whereas those with parents who continued the programme progressed even further.
- Training is intense and time-consuming, so it can be stressful for the family.
- Training is expensive as it involves intensive one-to-one treatment.

Summary

- Autism is a developmental disorder that starts early in childhood with impairment in three areas: social interaction, communication and restricted activities.
- Autistic children seem to have a particular deficit in 'joint attention'.
- Biological explanations for autism include genetics and neurological correlates.
- Cognitive explanations for autism include: lack of a theory of mind; central coherence deficit; failure of executive functioning.
- Common drug treatments used with autistic children include Risperidone.
- Behaviour modification is a process of shaping where small pieces of required behaviour are positively reinforced.
- It has been found that improvement is greater and better maintained when parents/caregivers are involved in a therapeutic programme.

Questions & Answers

About this section

In this section of the guide, there are six questions — two on social psychology, two on cognitive psychology and two on individual differences. Each question is worth 20 marks. You should allow 30 minutes when answering each question.

The section is structured as follows:

- sample questions in the style in which they appear on the Unit 2 examination paper
- analysis of each question, explaining what is expected in each sub-section of the question
- example student responses at the C/D-grade level (student A) — these have been selected to illustrate particular strengths and limitations
- example student responses at the A-grade level (student B) — such answers demonstrate thorough knowledge, a good understanding and an ability to deal with the data that are presented in the questions

Examiner's comments

All student responses are followed by examiners' comments. These are preceded by the icon e. They indicate where credit is due and, in the weaker answer, they also point out areas for improvement, specific problems and common errors such as poor time management, lack of clarity, weak or non-existent development, irrelevance, misinterpretation of the question and mistaken meanings of terms. The comments also indicate how each example answer would be marked in an actual exam.

The examination

The Unit 2 examination is 1 hour 30 minutes long and you have to answer questions on three topics: one social psychology, one cognitive psychology and one individual differences. Each question carries 20 marks, so you should allow 30 minutes for each.

All topic questions are structured, which means that there are several sub-sections for each topic. The first sub-sections are usually short-answer questions worth 1, 2, 3 or 4 marks. These are followed by a final sub-section, which requires extended writing for 10 marks.

Short-answer questions

- Commands such as 'identify', 'state', 'name', 'suggest' and 'give' require only the briefest of answers.
- Questions that contain commands such as 'outline' and 'describe' require straightforward descriptions.
- Verbs such as 'explain' and 'distinguish' indicate that some analysis or elaboration of concepts is required. In the case of 'distinguish', you need to explain the difference(s) between two concepts.

- The command 'briefly discuss' requires some description and some evaluation or criticism, and is usually worth 4 or 5 marks.
- If asked to 'describe a study' for 4 marks, you should refer explicitly to the aim, method, results and conclusion of the study.
- If asked to 'outline a study' for 2/3 marks, you should refer to the method/procedure and the results/findings.

Examples of short-answer questions

- *Identify* ***two*** *components of working memory.*
- *Explain what is meant by 'episodic memory'.*
- *Give an example of joint attention.*
- *State what is meant by a 'phobia'.*
- *Outline what psychologists mean by the term 'theory of mind'.*
- *Describe* ***one*** *study in which the Gestalt principles of perception were investigated.*
- *Briefly discuss* ***one*** *limitation of Gregory's theory of perception.*
- *Distinguish between internalisation and compliance.*

Long-answer questions

These are worth 10 marks. A typical 10-mark question would ask you to 'describe and evaluate' a theory, an explanation or some research. In 10-mark questions, 5 marks are for description and 5 are for evaluation/analysis/application. In the evaluation, you should present strengths and limitations. If relevant, you should support what you say with reference to evidence and explain how this relates to the topic. You can also get evaluation marks by comparing, for example introducing an opposing theory to illustrate the limitations of the theory that you are discussing. You should aim to spend plenty of time on this sub-section of the question in the examination.

In the 10-mark questions, you will be assessed on your ability to communicate. You should, therefore, make sure that your answer is properly structured into sentences and paragraphs, and pay attention to your spelling. If a 10-mark question asks you to 'refer to evidence' or 'refer to an alternative explanation', there will be a limit to the number of marks that you will be awarded if you do not comply with that instruction.

Mark schemes for 10-mark questions are banded into 'very good', 'good', 'average' and 'poor' bands, which means that the examiner will not only consider each individual point that you make, but will also make a global assessment of the answer as a whole. Students who show extensive knowledge and make many evaluation points but who do not present a well-argued response will sometimes be awarded a lower mark than they might have been given because the answer as a whole is better suited to the 'average' band than the 'good' band.

Scenario questions

In some questions, you must use your knowledge by applying what you have learned about psychology to a novel situation. For example, a question might include a scenario about someone who forgets in different situations. In this case, you might be required to use your knowledge of theories of forgetting to explain the experiences of the person in the scenario. For example, you could describe how decay theory could explain the person's forgetting because the event happened a long time ago. This sort of question tests the application of knowledge.

Assessment of practical psychology and research methods

In Unit 2, your knowledge of practical psychology and research methods will be tested in the context of the topic questions. For example, there may be a social influence question in which you are asked about a study of conformity that has been described to you. In this unit, you can only be asked about the experimental method, not about any other aspects of research methods. It is therefore crucial that you **cover the experimental method sub-section of Unit 1 before you take the Unit 2 examination**. The box below gives details of what you need to know about research methods for the Unit 2 examination. In any examination session, knowledge of the experimental method will be assessed in either **both** social questions, **both** cognitive questions or **both** individual differences questions.

Experimental methods

- experiments: field, laboratory and quasi-experiments
- issue of ecological validity
- independent and dependent variables; manipulation and control of variables in experiments; extraneous and confounding variables
- experimental designs: repeated or related measures, matched pairs, independent groups and appropriate use of each; controls associated with different designs, including counterbalancing and random allocation; strengths and limitations of different experimental designs
- strengths and limitations of experimental methods

Assessment objectives

Examination boards use the term 'assessment objective' (AO) to refer to the different types of skills that a student might be expected to demonstrate in examinations. Your teacher might have told you about AO1, AO2 and AO3 skills:

- AO1 refers to knowledge and understanding.
- AO2 refers to analysis and evaluation and to the application of knowledge to novel situations.
- AO3 refers to knowledge and understanding of research methods and practical psychology.

You should not worry too much about these different skills in the examination. In most cases, the wording of the question will lead you to demonstrate the necessary skills. Only the following two types of question require you to think about AO skills:

- 'Describe and evaluate' or 'Discuss' for 10 marks: whatever the wording of the 10-mark question, 5 marks are for description (AO1) and 5 marks are for evaluation, analysis and application (AO2). In a 10-mark question, you should aim to present balance of description and evaluation/analysis/application.
- 'Briefly discuss' for 3, 4 or 5 marks: here, there would normally be 1 or 2 marks for description (AO1) and 2 or 3 marks for evaluation, analysis and application (AO2).

Question 1 **Social psychology**

Social influence

(a) Outline what is meant by the following terms with respect to social facilitation:
(i) dominant responses (2 marks)
(ii) evaluation apprehension (2 marks)

ⓔ You need to state briefly what is meant by each of the two terms given, for 1 mark each. For the second mark, you should expand on the information by giving a little more detail for each term. Although an example relating to the term is not asked for, nor therefore required, it sometimes helps to clarify your outline if you do give an example. If it is an appropriate example and it does help the reader to understand the term, credit will be given.

(b) Joe was participating in a debate on nuclear power during a politics lesson. He had studied nuclear power in science and was strongly against it. He was surprised that his four friends were arguing in favour of nuclear power. When a vote was made, Joe found himself conforming to his friends and voting for nuclear power, even though he still privately disagreed with it.
(i) With reference to Joe, briefly discuss one reason why he might have conformed and voted with his friends in favour of nuclear power. (3 marks)
(ii) Identify and explain *one* factor that might have made Joe less likely to have conformed and voted with his friends in favour of nuclear power. (3 marks)

ⓔ The text provided before the questions should be read through carefully because it is there for you to refer to in your answer. Note that part (i) requires you to do several things. First, the question is 'briefly discuss', therefore you need to try to gain application, analysis or evaluation marks. Second, you are instructed to refer to Joe — if you do not do this, your marks will be restricted. The question also asks for one reason; it would be pointless to waste time discussing more than one reason as no credit would be given for extra reasons. This is a lot to think about for a short question, and it illustrates the necessity to read the questions carefully and work out exactly what is required prior to writing an answer. Part (ii) again asks for just *one* factor, so be careful to choose a factor that will enable you to gain further explanation marks.

(c) Describe and evaluate the authoritarian personality as an explanation for obedience. (10 marks)

ⓔ You are expected to show your knowledge of the authoritarian personality as an explanation for obedience by giving a clear and detailed description. Take care here because the authoritarian personality is also an explanation for prejudice, and although the two are linked, you should keep referring to '*obedience*' to ensure that you stay focused on the question set. Remember, it is always important to use any specialist terminology as it shows that you have been studying the topic. Half of the marks in these straightforward extended writing questions are for knowledge and description. The remaining marks are for evaluation, for example, by presenting strengths and limitations and using evidence to support what you say. Try to give a balanced discussion, not just criticisms, but also any strengths or backing evidence. Alternative explanations can be referred to, but make sure that they are linked to the question and answer — do not go off on a tangent, perhaps with an answer to the question that you had hoped would be asked!

Total: 20 marks

Student A

(a) (i) Dominant responses are those that dominate and we use all the time **a**.

(ii) Evaluation apprehension is when we think someone is assessing us and we start to work harder **b**. For example, if I am on the computer and my teacher stands behind me, I usually start to work faster. This is unless I am doing spreadsheets, which I am just learning and cannot do. If the teacher watches me do these, I make even more mistakes **c**.

e **(i) 0/2 marks awarded.** **a** Here the student uses the term 'dominate' to explain 'dominant', which is a common mistake. Although the student does express the essence of dominant responses, the answer is too vague to gain a mark because there is no indication that the dominant response can facilitate or inhibit performance.

e **(ii) 2/2 marks awarded.** **b** Evaluation apprehension refers to the feeling that we are being assessed or judged, and the example given helps to clarify this. **c** The student manages to convey the idea that evaluation apprehension can facilitate or inhibit performance by using an everyday example, i.e. when observed by the teacher, performance is improved, but when observed doing a task that is new or not well-practised (spreadsheets), performance is impaired. This is a good illustration of how using an example to explain a term can help gain the marks.

(b) (i) Joe might have conformed because all his friends thought that way. He would not like to have been left out. He might have thought that his friends would fall out with him and then he would be lonely **a**. This type of conformity is known as compliance — like Joe, you go along with it even though you disagree **b**.

e **2/3 marks awarded.** This is not a bad answer. The student has not used the term 'normative social influence', but the answer indicates that **a** Joe needs to be accepted by his friends and remain part of the group. **b** The type of conformity identified (compliance) is also correct and the student gains credit for identifying it accurately and linking it to Joe.

(ii) A number of factors were identified by Asch who did a study on conformity using lines. In this study participants had to say if one line was the same as one of the other three lines. This was a really easy task but other people were planted in the group and gave the wrong answer. This confused the participants so they, too, gave the wrong answer **c**. On this task they would give the correct answer if another person gave the correct answer. Studies have shown that if you can answer in a private booth, then you won't conform the same. However, these studies have been criticised **d**.

e **1/3 marks awarded.** This answer does not address the question set effectively. **c** There are no marks available for outlining Asch's study, so this part of the answer is surplus, and writing all this has wasted the student's time. The question asked for one factor and then an explanation of this factor. **d** This student has correctly identified two factors (lack of unanimity/presence of an ally and answering in private) but does not go on to explain either of the factors.

(c) Obedience is when a person acts in a particular way because an authority person has told him or her to **a**. Adorno suggested that certain people have very rigid personalities, which means they are not at all flexible and need to know the right answer because everything is black and white. These people are known as authoritarian personality **b**. They look up to people in higher authority than themselves and expect other people to do the same. Everyone should know their place and behave. This type of person is very obedient **c**. You can measure this type of personality with an F-scale for Fascist **d**. Fascists are very political and are people like the BNP. This type of person develops when they have been beaten or abused as a child.

There is some evidence that people who are high on the F questions are very obedient. In the Milgram study, these people gave much higher electric shocks to the learner than normal people **e**. But the questionnaire, or scale as it is sometimes called, that is used to measure Fascists can be criticised because it can mean everyone fills it in a set way because of the way the questions are. This is known as response set **f**.

e **6/10 marks awarded (AO1 = 4, AO2 = 2).** The answer is well organised and, although it is not written very clearly, the points made are discernible and the description is focused and largely accurate. However, the evaluation and analysis are weak. The following four points are awarded marks for description: **a** the basic definition of obedience; **b** the link between authoritarian personality and rigidity; **c** the link between submissiveness and obedience (although 'submissiveness' was not used as a term, the explanation makes this clear); **d** the knowledge that this personality type can be measured with the F-scale. These points gain 4 of the 5 AO1 marks available. Evaluation marks are awarded for the following two points: **e** the first point about people who score high on the F-scale giving higher levels of shock on the Milgram study (although not well stated, it is worthy of AO2 credit); **f** the second point about the methodological problem with the F-scale (it is reasonably clear and the student remembers the correct term at the end), which is worthy of AO2 credit.

Total for this question: 11/20 marks — approximately grade C/D

Student B

(a) (i) The term 'dominant response' refers to the behaviours that we are most likely to perform in a situation **a**. If a person is very skilled — say a premier football player — then the dominant response is to play well, and this response is likely to be enhanced when spectators are present. Conversely, on a skill that is not as well practised, say the footballer is playing in an unusual position, then the dominant response may be to play less well and spectators would inhibit performance **b**.

(ii) Evaluation apprehension refers to the fact that when we are observed by others, we feel that we are being judged and that others are evaluating our performance **c**. The observation by others creates arousal in us and this can facilitate easy tasks and inhibit more difficult tasks **d**.

e **(i) and (ii) 4/4 marks awarded.** **a c d** Here the student outlines both terms fully and **b** the example (although not asked for) is used well to clarify the explanation of a dominant response.

(b) (i) Although Joe is against nuclear fuel, he seems to be the only one among his friends thinking like this. Joe will want to fit in with the group and will not like to be seen as different or be rejected by them, particularly as this is an important reference group. This type of conformity is known as normative social influence and is based on the need to be accepted by others **a**. Even though Joe privately still holds his own view, publicly he goes along with the group **b**, and this is compliance **c**.

e **3/3 marks awarded.** This is a good answer. The student has used appropriate terminology, e.g. **a** 'normative social influence', and **b** the answer refers appropriately to Joe and his need to be accepted by his friends and remain part of the group. **c** The type of conformity identified (compliance) is also correct and the student gains credit for accurately identifying it and linking it to Joe.

(ii) Psychologists have identified a number of factors that might decrease conformity. One factor is unanimity **d**. In an experiment by Asch, conformity decreased if one other participant gave the correct answer prior to the naïve participant **e**. In the debate about nuclear power, this would mean that, if one of Joe's friends had argued against the use of nuclear power, Joe would have been more likely to speak his mind and not conform **f**.

e **3/3 marks awarded.** **d** The factor identified (unanimity) is appropriate and the discussion **f** links both to the text and **e** to research by Asch in a relevant way.

(c) Obedience is when a person acts in a particular way due to an order from an authority figure. Psychologists have proposed a number of explanations for obedience, some to do with the situation (e.g. as investigated by Milgram) and some to do with the personality of the individual. Explanations concerned with the individual's personality are known as dispositional explanations, and Adorno et al. (1950) proposed an explanation for obedience based on the authoritarian personality type of the individual **a**.

The authoritarian personality type is submissive to those of higher status and expects others to be the same. They are deferential to authority and they expect others to be obedient to authority too. They are quite hostile and scathing of those they believe to be 'below' them. They do not like uncertainty and are quite rigid and inflexible in their thinking and behaviour. The authoritarian individual is very conventional and highly political, usually extremely right-wing **a**.

The F- (for Fascist) scale is a scale developed by Adorno to measure authoritarianism and contains statements such as 'Leaders should be strict with people to gain respect' and 'Children should learn obedience' **a**. The development of this type of personality was thought to be due to childhood experiences, and explanations draw on Freud's theory of personality. Children who have been abused or suffered hardship are more likely to be authoritarian as adults and demand obedience from others **a**.

There is evidence for Adorno's theory, some of it based on experiments on obedience. Milgram carried out a series of experiments on obedience where a 'learner' was given an electric shock by a 'teacher'. The teachers thought that they were administering shocks, and 65% carried on giving shocks up to 450 volts because an authority figure told them to do so. Milgram found a strong positive correlation between the authoritarian personality type and giving shocks up to the maximum voltage **b**. This would be predicted by the authoritarian personality theory, as these individuals are more obedient to authority **b**. However, there are problems with applying Adorno's theory to a large population because his original sample was small **b**. The scale itself has been criticised because all the statements are in one direction and thus it is open to response set. This is where participants simply respond in a similar way to each statement, irrespective of what it reads. For example, they might always tick 'agree' and this would give them a high score and therefore mean that they would be a strong authoritarian type **b**. This is a problem for the scale because it makes it unreliable **b**.

e **10/10 marks awarded (AO1 = 5, AO2 = 5).** This is a comprehensive answer that both describes the theory well and offers appropriate evaluation points that are thoroughly discussed. It is a balanced answer with both strengths (in the form of evidence) and weaknesses associated with the theory and research into the authoritarian personality. **a** The definition and link to 'disposition' in the first paragraph is creditworthy. **a** The descriptive points in the second paragraph with regard to the personality type gain AO1 credit, **a** as does the knowledge of the F-scale in the third paragraph. **a** There is a reference to how this personality type develops with respect to Freud, which is nicely linked back to obedience. **b** The AO2 credit comes largely from the last paragraph and it is heartening to see that the student has not just stated the evaluative point but attempted to offer a discussion. This is quite sophisticated for this level and something that better students are capable of doing. All the discussion is relevant, uses appropriate terminology and is largely clear and accurate. There is no evidence of misunderstanding, and the answer includes some well-argued evaluation and analysis. This is a top-band answer.

Total for this question: 20/20 — grade A

Question 2 **Social psychology**

Social cognition

(a) Josh and Jack were late for class. At the end of the lesson, the teacher asked Jack why he had been late. He said, 'The alarm did not go off this morning.' When she asked Jack if he knew why Josh was late, he said, 'Josh is very lazy.'
(i) Identify and explain the type of attribution bias in this example. Refer to the remarks made by Jack to his teacher. (3 marks)
(ii) Name *one other* attribution bias. (1 marks)

e Part (i) is asking you to identify an attribution bias for 1 mark. The other 2 marks are gained for the explanation of that attribution bias and for correctly relating this bias to the explanations that Jack gave for his own and Josh's lateness. In part (ii), there is only a requirement to name one other attribution bias.

(b) Name and briefly explain *two* factors affecting impression formation. (6 marks)

e You would gain 2 marks for naming any two factors affecting impression formation — these are just knowledge marks. The explanation requires an expansion and analysis of these factors, which is more difficult. You should try to assess how each factor you have identified affects impression formation. Although not specifically asked for, an example (of your own or from a study) might aid the explanation.

(c) Describe and evaluate the structural approach to attitudes. Refer to empirical evidence in your answer. (10 marks)

e You are expected to show your knowledge of the structural approach by offering a clear description. Remember, it is always important to use any specialist terminology, as this shows that you have been studying the topic. Half of the marks in these straightforward extended writing questions are for knowledge and description. The remaining marks are for evaluation, i.e. presenting strengths and limitations and using evidence to support what you say. It is possible to gain evaluation marks by referring to an alternative approach, but this must be linked clearly to the question set. For example, you could discuss the fact that the structural approach concentrates on the structural components of attitudes but does not assess the function that these attitudes hold, whereas the functional approach does. In this question you are required to 'refer to empirical evidence' in your answer. It is important to remember that if you fail to comply with any instruction asking you to refer to evidence, you will gain only a maximum of 6 marks, however good the rest of your answer may be.

Total: 20 marks

Student A

(a) (i) This is the actor–observer bias **a**, where we explain our own behaviour according to something within us and other people are explained because of the situation, i.e. Jack says Josh is lazy **b**.

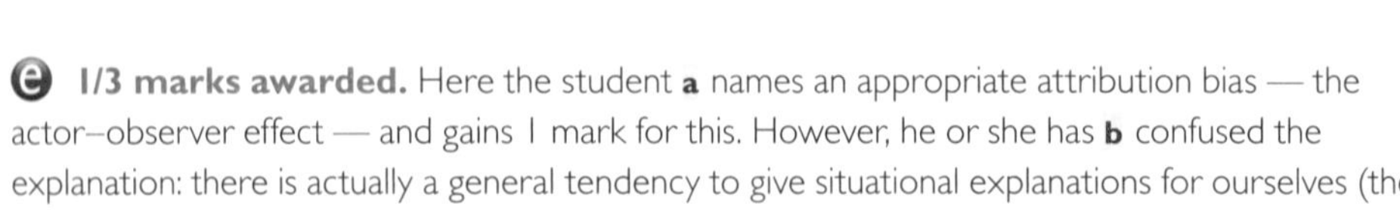

e **1/3 marks awarded.** Here the student **a** names an appropriate attribution bias — the actor–observer effect — and gains 1 mark for this. However, he or she has **b** confused the explanation: there is actually a general tendency to give situational explanations for ourselves (the alarm did not go off) and dispositional reasons for other people (Josh is lazy).

(ii) The fundamental error (FAE) **c**.

e **1/1 mark awarded.** **c** This is a correct alternative attribution bias and, although the student missed the word 'attribution' out of the answer, it is obvious that this is the bias that he or she is referring to.

(b) A number of factors affect impression formation, such as the primacy and recency effects **a** and stereotyping **b**. The primacy/recency is like memory and that study where people were given a list of words that they had to recall is a good example of this. In this study people could recall the words from the beginning of the list and words from the end. The middle of the list was in 'no man's land'. These words may never get anywhere **c**.

Stereotyping affects the impression we form of other people because we have expectations of what certain people will behave like, such as girls cry a lot **d**.

e **3/6 marks awarded.** The first sentence **a b** identifies a number of factors accurately and gains the 2 marks for identification. **c** The student then seems to get 'off track' a little by outlining the primacy and recency effects with respect to memory. Although this is not totally unrelated to social cognition, the student fails to make the 'social' link, therefore this explanation does not gain any marks. The last sentence on stereotyping is quite good because it expands on the knowledge of stereotypes and refers to expectations. However, the example is not linked back to impressions formed and is not sufficient to gain another mark. So although not well explained, the explanation of stereotyping gains a mark for the idea of expectation and for girls crying as a type of stereotyping **d**.

(c) The structural approach to attitudes says that attitudes have three parts known as A B C **a**. The A is affect and is to do with emotion, how we feel about something. So if it is a cat, the affective part would be if we liked the cat. B stands for behaviour and this is how we behave towards the cat. Do we stroke it and say nice things to it, or do we kick it and throw it out of the house all the time? C stands for? and is what we know about or believe about cats, such as believing cats are good company **a**. This approach to attitudes says that these three parts, A B C, are usually consistent, which means they usually all agree. For example, if we feel we like cats we usually know good things about them and stroke them and care for them well **a**. Some studies, however, show that the opposite is true such as the study when the Chinese couple couldn't get into hotels and restaurants when they telephoned to ask, but when they turned up people let them in and were kind to them **b**.

The functional approach to attitudes is concerned with the function of an attitude held by an individual, for example whether it is knowledge or ego **c**.

6/10 marks awarded (AO1 = 5, AO2 = 1). The answer starts off fairly well and gives a reasonable description of the three components of an attitude according to the structural approach. The example helps to clarify the points being made about the three components. There is a good point about consistency and very little inaccuracy or irrelevance in the first paragraph. The five descriptive marks have been accrued for knowledge of the structural approach as follows: **a** knowledge that there are three components; **a** identification of each component; **a** factual knowledge on consistency. The student also makes a reasonable attempt to offer an evaluative comment about the LaPiere study. **b** It is not detailed, nor is it perfect, but the point made about inconsistency is a valid one and deserving of an AO2 mark (note also that the question requires reference to a study, and this is a good one to choose). This student has forgotten that 'C' stands for 'cognitive', but this does not detract from the answer because this component is accurately outlined and, clearly, the student has sound knowledge of this. **c** The final sentence about the functional approach is not tied in to the question in any way and is completely redundant. It could have been used in an evaluative way, but as it stands it gains no points.

Total for this question: 11/20 — approximately grade C/D

Student B

(a) (i) Jack is showing an actor–observer effect **a** because he explains his own behaviour according to the situation (his alarm did not go off this morning) and yet when asked about his friend Josh, he explains his friend's behaviour according to his disposition, stating that Josh is lazy **b**.

3/3 marks awarded. **a** Here the student names an appropriate attribution bias — the actor–observer effect — and gains 1 mark for this. **b** The answer clearly explains this bias as one where we are more likely to attribute the cause of our own behaviour to the situation but the cause of someone else's behaviour to disposition. In addition, the student accurately applies the answer to the text offered at the beginning of the question.

(ii) The fundamental attribution error **c**.

1/1 mark awarded. **c** This is a correct alternative attribution bias.

(b) The primacy effect **a**, the recency effect, stereotyping **a** and social schemas all affect the impression we form of other people. The primacy effect is where what we hear/see first about a person affects how we perceive him or her **b**. In an interview, for example, if the interviewee makes a poor first impression, perhaps by wearing inappropriate clothes or making a thoughtless comment, then it is difficult to change the impression formed of that person. Asch carried out a study and found that if participants are asked to rate a person after being given six traits, a more positive rating would be given if the traits were presented with the positive things first (e.g. intelligent, industrious, impulsive...) than when presented with the same traits but the negative ones first (e.g. envious, stubborn, critical, impulsive...). The recency effect is the opposite of the primacy effect and is the finding that information we encounter last is more influential. This finding is not as strong as the primacy effect **c**.

Stereotyping is when we are biased and interpret things in a particular way because we believe that members of a group share similar traits **d**. For example, we have stereotypes about accents and may think that people with a Liverpudlian accent do not want to work, and therefore our impression of a Liverpudlian that we do meet will be interpreted in this biased way **e**. We also have stereotypes about particular races. We may hold a stereotype that Japanese people are cruel and then interpret all Japanese people in this way.

e 6/6 marks awarded. **a** The first sentence identifies a number of factors accurately and this gains the 2 marks for identification (note, however, that the answer goes beyond what is required and names more than two factors). **b** The student gains 2 marks for the explanation of the primacy effect. The student then goes on to **c** outline and explain the recency effect. The level of detail is too much for 2 marks and the student could jeopardise his or her performance on the examination overall because he or she has spent too much time on this short question. This is a common mistake. Students should read the question carefully and then write an appropriate amount. For this question, it is clearly 3 marks for each factor and, as it states 'identify', one of the marks will be for the identification of the factor. This means that there are only 2 marks available for the explanation, so the student could gain these marks with a much shorter answer. **a b** Nevertheless, he or she does gain all the marks for this first factor. **c** The recency effect could be taken as a second factor but is not well explained, therefore the second factor is taken to be **d** 'stereotyping'. **e** This answer is not as extensive as for the first factor, but is certainly sufficient to gain the full marks. There is no requirement to use an example, but **e** the example provided does help to explain the concept and is credited. However, there is certainly no need to use two examples to clarify the explanation.

(c) According to the structural approach to attitudes, attitudes contain three components **a**. One component is the behavioural component and this is the part of the attitude that we show through our behaviour to a particular person/object/idea etc **a**. For example, if we do not like spiders, we would run away or jump on a chair when we saw one. The second component of an attitude is the affective component, which is how we feel. We would tell people that we feel scared of spiders and don't like them. The third component is the cognitive component, and this is what we know and believe about an object. For example, we might believe that a spider is harmful and know that it can run very fast and might bite. Some spiders, we may believe, are poisonous **a**. The structural approach to attitudes predicts that the components of an attitude act in a consistent way, therefore what we believe and feel about a spider will be reflected in our behaviour. Studies have been done to assess the consistency of attitudes **a**. LaPiere visited a number of restaurants and hotels in America to find out if they would accept the Chinese race in their establishments. At the time, there was prejudice against the Chinese race in America. When they visited the establishments, only one place refused them admission and they were treated politely at the others. However, when contacted 6 months later, 90% of the places said they would not allow Chinese people to stay there. In other words, there was an inconsistency between what people said and what they did, and this does not support the idea that the structural approach suggests, that the components are usually consistent **b**. One note of caution about the results from this study is that it was in 1934 and such open racial prejudice may no longer be evident **b**. One criticism of the structural approach to attitudes is that it tells us nothing about the functions that attitudes serve, and therefore for a more complete theory of attitudes, it is probably better to consider both the structural and functional approaches **b**. The functional approach is also a more useful approach when attempting to change attitudes **b**.

e **10/10 marks awarded (AO1 = 5, AO2 = 5).** The answer is long and more detailed than is strictly necessary. Nevertheless, this is a student who knows a lot of information and gets it onto paper quickly. **a** A thorough description of the three components of an attitude according to the structural approach is covered. **a** The examples given help to clarify the points being made about these components. **a** There is a good point about consistency and no inaccuracy or irrelevance in the first paragraph. AO1 credit has been accrued for **a** knowledge of the three components, **a** identification of each component and **a** factual knowledge on consistency. **a** The student describes the LaPiere study succinctly and reasonably accurately, and this would gain further AO1 credit for description if the student needed further AO1 points. This study satisfies the demands of the question to refer to evidence and so is able to gain above the 6-mark limit. **b** There are also plenty of evaluative comments that gain the necessary AO2 credit. For example, we are informed that the LaPiere study assesses the consistency theory of the structural model, **b** and then finds it wanting. The mention of how the findings are dated is also worthy of AO2 credit, and **b** the functional approach is clearly linked to the question and used in an evaluative manner. Overall, this is an excellent answer.

Total for this question: 20/20 — grade A.

Question 3 **Cognitive psychology**

Remembering and forgetting

(a) Sunayna has been learning French for 3 years but has now got a job in Spain. She is having difficulty learning Spanish and keeps mixing up her Spanish and French words.

Name and explain *one* type of forgetting that might be causing Sunayna's difficulty in learning this new language. (2 marks)

ⓔ You are required to do two things and you would get a mark for each. First, you need to name a suitable theory of forgetting. Second, you need to explain the named theory with respect to Sunayna attempting to learn a new language. Make sure that you select a suitable theory that fits with the context.

(b) Outline *one* criticism of the theory of forgetting that you have explained in your answer to part (a). (2 marks)

ⓔ You have to ensure that you link your answer to the theory referred to in part (a) of this question. The first mark is for a relevant criticism outlined briefly, and the second mark is for an expansion or further relevant details relating to the same criticism.

(c) Ten participants were asked to process 20 words (common nouns such as 'CAR') one at a time with a 5-second interval between each word. For ten words, participants had to think of an adjective to describe each word (e.g. for 'CAR' an adjective might be 'blue') — this is deep/semantic processing. For the other ten words, participants had to decide whether the word was in capital letters or not — this is shallow/structural processing. Previous research has found poorer recall when words are processed at a shallow level. The results are presented in the table below.

	Deep processing ('adjective' condition)	**Shallow processing ('capital letter' condition)**
Mean number of words recalled out of ten	8	5

(i) Identify the independent and dependent variables in this study. (2 marks)
(ii) Name and outline the experimental design used in this study. (2 marks)
(iii) Identify and outline one potential confounding variable in this study. (2 marks)

ⓔ This is testing your knowledge of practical psychology. You need to read the details in the text carefully so that you understand the study. You may already be familiar with the experiment from your study of memory, but knowledge of the study is not necessary. Part (i) is for 2 marks and requires you to identify the IV and DV. Remember to be as clear about this as possible, saying exactly what is being manipulated in the two conditions and exactly what is being measured. In part (ii), you are required to do two things (1 mark each): name the experimental design and offer an explanation of what it involves. In part (iii), 1 mark is for identifying an appropriate confounding variable, and the second mark is for outlining the effect that it would have on the results if it was not controlled.

(d) Describe and evaluate research into the multi-store model of memory. **(10 marks)**

ⓔ This is not as straightforward as it might first appear. It is a question on the multi-store model, but on careful reading it should be clear that the emphasis of the question is on 'research'. You are expected to show your knowledge of research by offering a clear description of relevant studies, and this knowledge and description is worth half of the marks. The remaining marks are for evaluation, i.e. presenting strengths and limitations of the studies. These marks can be gained by explaining how well the research supports the model. Alternative models can be referred to but must be made relevant to the question. Simply describing and evaluating the multi-store model without reference to research will not be creditworthy.

Total: 20 marks

Student A

(a) Sunayna might be getting interference between the French she has already learned and the new language **a**.

ⓔ **1/2 marks awarded.** **a** The student has correctly identified an appropriate theory of forgetting but the answer is brief and does not really explain how the interference might occur. For example, the student could say that there is proactive interference because the French language she has already learned may be coming forward and interfering with the Spanish that she is attempting to learn now.

(b) Studies into interference have usually been experiments and these lack ecological validity **a**.

ⓔ **1/2 marks awarded.** **a** Here the student has made two points, both of which are valid and could refer to interference theory, but the criticism is not fully outlined. Why experiments lack ecological validity is not explained, and therefore it is not clear why this is a criticism.

(c) (i) The independent variable is the level of processing (whether it is deep or shallow) **a**. The dependent variable is the words **b**.

ⓔ **1/2 marks awarded.** This answer is not sufficient to gain the full 2 marks. **a** The IV is sufficiently clearly stated, but the **b** DV is too vague for a mark. Remember to state exactly what it is that will be measured.

(ii) This is a repeated measures design **c**. This is because the same participants are doing both the shallow processing and the deep processing condition **d**. This design is good because you do not have any individual differences, but the problem is counterbalancing **e**.

ⓔ **2/2 marks awarded.** This answer gets the full 2 marks for correctly **c** naming and **d** explaining the relevant design. However, **e** the last sentence is redundant because the question does not ask for any evaluation.

(iii) This was a study on memory, and therefore a confounding variable would be length of words **f**. To control for this, words should all be the same length.

ⓔ **1/2 marks awarded. f** 'Length of words' would possibly be a confounding variable in this study, but the answer does not outline why this might confound the results. For example, it could have outlined that longer words might be harder to recall because they take more time to process. This answer gains a mark for identifying a potential confounding variable, but not the second mark for outlining it.

(d) The multi-store model of memory was proposed by Atkinson and Shiffrin and it states that there are three types of memory. The first is a sensory memory and this holds information for a very short period of time before it is lost or goes to another memory store called short-term memory. This memory can hold about seven things, like seven numbers or names, and when extra things are added, the information is pushed out. This is called displacement and is a theory of forgetting in short-term memory. Another theory of forgetting is trace decay. There is evidence for the displacement of information from short-term memory. For example, if a study is done where people are given 20 words, then they remember the first few and the last few **a**. This is called the primacy/recency effect. They do not remember the middle words because these have been pushed out of short-term memory — because it only holds seven things. There is also a long-term memory store in this model.

Lots of studies have been done on this model. Baddeley did a study that proved that short-term memory holds information in an acoustic code and that long-term memory has a semantic code **b**. Paterson also did a study that showed that the duration of short-term memory was about 80 seconds **c**. He gave participants trigrams such as YBG and asked them to recall after 3 seconds and then up to 30 seconds at intervals. But these studies have been criticised because they lack ecological validity **d**. The model has also been criticised by the working memory model, because this model states that short-term memory has many stores **d**.

ⓔ **4/10 marks awarded (AO1 = 3, AO2 = 1).** The answer does not address the question well at all. It has not focused on research, particularly in the first part, and when it does eventually address some research, this is done in a cursory way. There is **a** some description of the 'primacy/recency' experiment that is worthy of (AO1) credit. The study by **b** Baddeley is not described but the results did lead to the conclusion stated and this is worthy of further credit. **c** However, there is some inaccuracy in the brief description of the 'Paterson' (probably Peterson and Peterson) study and this is worthy of just 1 mark, mainly for the knowledge of trigrams and link to duration of STM. **d** There are two brief evaluative comments at the end, neither of which on its own would gain a mark, but which, together, may be worthy of AO2 credit. Overall, this is an answer that is long but full of irrelevance and that never really answers the question set.

Total for this question: 10/20 — approximately grade D.

Student B

(a) Sunayna has learned French first and this is probably interfering with her attempts to learn Spanish now **a**. She is forgetting her new Spanish words perhaps because of proactive interference **a**, where information learned earlier comes forward and interferes with present learning **b**.

e **2/2 marks awarded.** Here the student proposes an **a** appropriate explanation of Sunayna's forgetting and **b** explains how proactive interference works.

(b) It is difficult to investigate interference as a theory of forgetting under controlled conditions, and studies that have been carried out generally resort to learning lists of words **a**. This type of investigation is artificial, and interference may be a theory that is demonstrated in the laboratory but not that relevant to real life, so the research lacks ecological validity **b**.

e **2/2 marks awarded.** **a** This is a valid criticism and it is **b** fully outlined.

(c) (i) The IV is whether the participants are asked semantic questions for deep processing or about the letter case for shallow processing **a**. The dependent variable is the number of words correctly recalled out of ten **b**.

e **2/2 marks awarded.** Both the **a** IV and **b** DV are correctly and fully operationalised.

(ii) The design of the study is repeated measures **c**, meaning that the same people take part in the two conditions and afterwards their performances are compared **d**.

e **2/2 marks awarded.** The design is **c** identified correctly and **d** explained clearly.

(iii) One potential confounding variable in this study is noise **e**. Because it is a memory study, if the noise level is too high when some participants are doing one condition of the study, then they would not be able to concentrate or even hear the words and this may affect their results and they may perform poorly **f**.

e **2/2 marks awarded.** **e** This is an appropriate confounding variable that has been identified, and the **f** outline is thorough enough to gain the second mark.

(d) The multi-store model of memory proposes that there is both a short-term store (STM) and a long-term store (LTM), and that information that enters sensory memory can be passed to STM and rehearsed. If information is rehearsed often enough, it will be transferred to LTM. The evidence for the properties associated with the different types of store comes largely from experiments. Miller (1956) found evidence for the STM having a capacity of between five and nine items, whereas LTM can store potentially an infinite amount of material **a**. The duration of STM is approximately 18 seconds, and this was established by Peterson and Peterson (1959) **a**. They gave participants trigrams and a distracter task to prevent rehearsal for varying lengths of time from 3 seconds to 30 seconds. They found that after 18 seconds, 80% of material had been lost from STM and therefore established that this was the duration of STM. Clearly, this is much shorter than the duration of LTM, as we remember some things forever **a**. Also, Baddeley found evidence that STM had an acoustic code whereas LTM had a semantic code **a**. The different properties associated with STM and LTM suggest that they really are separate stores **b**. However, much of the research that has been carried out has been controlled experiments that offer reliability and can establish cause and effect, **b** but may lack ecological validity. This is because any findings may not represent how memory works in the real world. Indeed, some studies have shown that with practice, STM can be extended, such as the work by Neisser and his study of waitresses taking orders, who had no difficulty rehearsing up to 18 different drinks **b**. Further evidence for the multi-store model comes from studies of patients suffering from amnesia. Case studies, such as the study of HM who had a brain operation for severe epilepsy, have shown that STM can be damaged but LTM remain intact, suggesting the two stores must indeed be separate **b**.

e **10/10 marks awarded (AO1= 5, AO2 = 5).** This is an extremely thorough answer that meets all the requirements of the question set. It both describes relevant research into the multi-store model of memory and offers some evaluation of the research. The student has not spent too long on the description of the model (as weaker students might): he or she has outlined briefly the main components to 'set the scene' so that research evidence can be discussed. **a** The factual information about the properties of the different components, together with the research by Miller, Peterson and Peterson, Baddeley and Neisser and the case study of HM have accumulated all the required descriptive (AO1) credit. **b** The point made about the different properties providing evidence for distinct and separate stores is a sophisticated evaluative comment and worthy of AO2 credit. Both the strength and weakness discussed in relation to the use of experiments are quite brief but adequately expressed and worthy of AO2 credit. **a b** The use of the case study and the Neisser study illustrate good discussion. This is an excellent answer given the time limitations.

Total for this question: 20/20 — grade A.

Question 4 **Cognitive psychology**

Perceptual processes

(a) Name *two* Gestalt principles of perceptual organisation. (2 marks)

ⓔ You are required to simply name two Gestalt principles and you would get a mark for each.

(b) Outline *one* criticism of Gestalt principles of perceptual organisation. (2 marks)

ⓔ You need to think of a suitable criticism. Choose one for which you think you can gain a second mark by expanding on the first point. Be careful, this may not be the first criticism that comes to mind. It is important to try to access both points, particularly on these short questions, if you are to gain a top grade.

(c) To test the effect of emotion on perceptual set, a group of ten participants were recruited by opportunity sampling. Each participant was presented with a list of 20 words, one at a time, and had to name the word as soon as it was recognised. Half of the words were neutral (e.g. apple, cat) and half of the words were emotional (e.g. blood, gun). Previous research had shown that the recognition threshold for emotional words was much longer than for neutral words. The results are presented in the table below.

Time taken in seconds	Emotional words	Neutral words
Mean (seconds)	36	14

(i) Identify the independent and dependent variables in this study. (2 marks)

(ii) Identify *one* possible extraneous variable in this study and explain how it might have affected the results if it was not controlled. (2 marks)

(iii) Name the experimental design used in this study and give one advantage of using this design in this case. (2 marks)

ⓔ This is testing your knowledge of practical psychology. You need to read the details in the text carefully so that you understand the study. You may already be familiar with the experiment from your study of perceptual processes, but knowledge of the study is not necessary. In part (i), you would get 1 mark for correctly stating the IV and 1 mark for the DV. Remember, these should be defined (operationalised) in as much detail as possible. In part (ii), you are required to identify a possible extraneous variable and say what effect it might have on the results if not controlled. In part (iii), 1 mark is for identifying the relevant design, and the other mark is for noting an advantage of this type of design in relation to the present study.

(d) Discuss what distortion illusions and ambiguous figures tell us about perception. (10 marks)

The wording is directly from the specification and so it should not be a surprise. However, it is quite an open question so you should plan your answer carefully. Remember, it is always important to use any specialist terminology as it shows that you have been studying the topic. Terms such as 'top-down', 'active processing', 'hypothesis testing' and 'perceptual set' could be used with respect to ambiguous figures and visual illusions. Think of an ambiguous figure that you can use as an example — the Necker cube and Rubin's vase are named on the specification, but you could refer to others. With respect to visual illusions, Müller-Lyer and Ponzo are on the specification, and terminology such as 'size constancy', 'depth cues' etc. could be used and linked to one (or more) specific illusions. In such an exam question, it is useful to keep referring back to the question set, perhaps rephrasing it in your own words, for example: 'Explain what these things tell us about visual perception'. Remember, too, that some evaluative comment will be required in your answer.

Total: 20 marks

Student A

(a) Gestalt psychologists say 'the whole is greater than the sum of parts' **a**. They are also interested in how we group similar things together **b**.

e **2/2 marks awarded.** Here the student gives a major **a** assumption of the Gestalt approach with the first sentence. This is worthy of a mark. The second mark is for the **b** grouping of similar things and this is one of the principles that are most likely to be given. Others include 'proximity', 'closure' etc.

(b) The Gestalt laws describe a two-dimensional world — we live in a three-dimensional world **a**.

e **1/2 marks awarded. a** The actual criticism is left fairly covert in this answer: it is not clear why this is a criticism of perceptual organisation. If the student had gone on to say that the world around us is three-dimensional and therefore the two-dimensional laws are limited in what they can explain, this criticism would be worthy of both marks.

(c) (i) The IV is the words **a** and the DV is also the words **b**.

e **0/2 marks awarded.** Neither the **a** IV nor the **b** DV is adequately identified, so this answer gets no marks.

(ii) One extraneous variable is the time taken to see each word **c**. If they had longer to look at one word than another, then this would affect the recall **d**.

e **0/2 marks awarded.** The student has chosen an **c** inappropriate extraneous variable. In this study the time limit could not be controlled by the researcher because the whole point of the research is to see how long it takes participants to recognise each word. Notice, too, how the answer refers to the way this might affect **d** 'recall', when in fact the experiment is not about recall at all. This student clearly has not read the question carefully enough.

(iii) The experiment is a repeated measures design **e**. This is useful for this experiment because it gets rid of any individual differences, for example if one person has worse eyesight than another, then this might affect how long it takes them **f**.

e **2/2 marks awarded.** This answer gains both marks because the **e** design given is correct and the **f** advantage of using this design in the present study is clear.

(d) Visual illusions and ambiguous figures are important because from them psychologists have learned that perception is an active process **a**. This means that our brain is trying to make sense of sensory input and we are affected by what we expect **b**. For example, when we look at a figure such as Rubin's vase, we are likely to see the faces if we look at pictures of faces beforehand. This is because we have been 'set' to see a particular thing and our perception has been influenced. Visual illusions such as the Müller-Lyer tell psychologists a lot because they have depth cues **c**. These are in the arrows and when psychologists move the arrows the depth cues change. They can discover how these processes work and it has led people like Gregory to suggest a top-down theory of perception **d**. However, a lot of the work that Gregory and others have carried out has been on drawings and not the real world and this may not be valid **e**.

e **6/10 marks awarded (AO1 = 5, AO2 = 1).** The answer is brief and the points made are not always explained fully, but there are a number of important concepts covered. The material tries to answer the question set and at least the student does not fall into the trap that many do, which is writing everything they know about illusions and ambiguous figures. Two examples have been given, which are correct and worthy of AO1 credit. The opening sentence is good and would gain AO1 credit for the concept of **a** perception as an active process. **b** The idea of expectation is also a good point and fairly well presented, although the opportunity to develop the material has not been taken AO1 credit is gained. **c** There is some knowledge of depth cues giving information to psychologists. It is not well explained but, **d** together with the idea of Gregory's top-down approach, is worthy of some credit. **e** The evaluation is cursory and is worthy of AO2 limited credit. This answer is knowledgeable at the descriptive level but lacks any in-depth analysis and evaluation.

Total for this question: 11/20 — approximately grade C/D

Student B

(a) [] [] X X [] [] X X
[] [] X X [] [] X X
[] [] X X [] [] X X

Gestalt psychologists have a number of laws or principles, and these include the law of closure **a**, where we tend to close figures up to make a whole, and the law of similarity where similar things are seen in a group together **b**. In the diagram above, we tend to close up the boxes and see columns of boxes and Xs rather than rows.

e **2/2 marks awarded.** Here the student gives two appropriate laws — **a** closure and **b** similarity. Although the examples are not required, they are permissible and sometimes a diagram helps to clarify the text. (However, on their own, without any explanation, diagrams do not usually gain marks.)

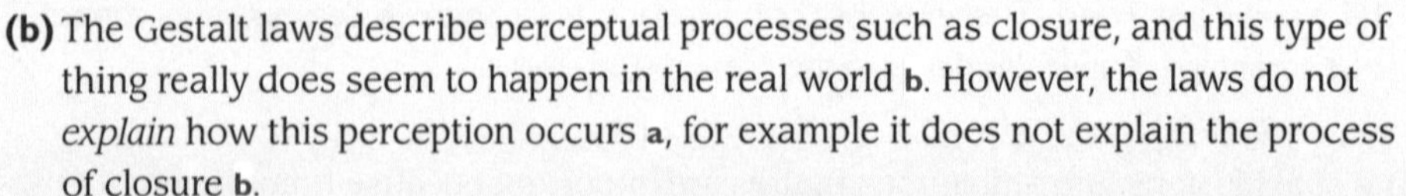

(b) The Gestalt laws describe perceptual processes such as closure, and this type of thing really does seem to happen in the real world **b**. However, the laws do not *explain* how this perception occurs **a**, for example it does not explain the process of closure **b**.

e **2/2 marks awarded.** This is a **a** valid criticism of the perceptual laws of organisation, and the student has attempted to **b** expand with an example of what the law of closure describes but does not explain.

(c) (i) The IV is whether the words are emotionally connected or neutral **a**. The DV is how long it takes in seconds to state the words **b**.

e **2/2 marks awarded.** Both the **a** IV and the **b** DV are correct.

(ii) One possible extraneous variable would be the way the words are presented **c**. For example, if some words were in blacker ink than others, these would be recognised more quickly whether or not they were emotional words **d**.

e **2/2 marks awarded.** A sensible extraneous variable is **c** identified for the first mark, and the student gains the second mark because he or she **d** explains how this variable might affect the results if not controlled.

(iii) In this case the researcher uses a repeated design **e**. This is a good design to use here so that there are no participant variables. In a repeated design, you compare the same person with him- or herself in both conditions, so you can be certain that a difference is due to the type of word and not to the person being someone else **f**.

e **2/2 marks awarded.** The student **e** identifies the correct design for 1 mark and gives **f** an advantage that is clearly linked to the present study for the second mark.

(d) A distortion illusion is where our perceptual system is 'tricked' into thinking that something is different from the actual retinal information **a**. For example, one visual illusion is the Ponzo illusion (see below), where two converging vertical lines seem to make horizontal lines appear different lengths even though they are the same size. This is because the converging lines give off depth cues suggesting that the top horizontal line is further away.

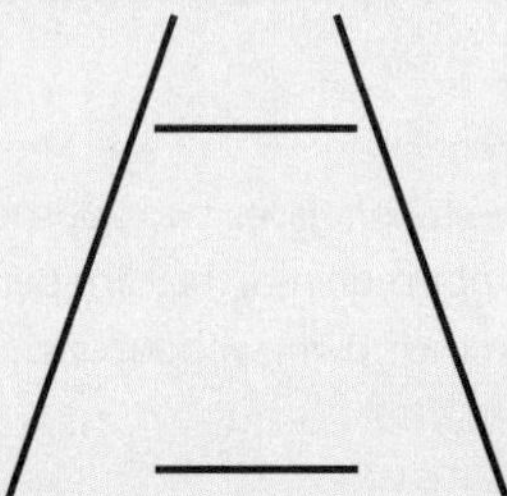

Ambiguous figures give off two hypotheses about a stimulus, and the same input results in different perceptions **a**. Rubin's vase is an example of an ambiguous figure that can be viewed as a vase or two faces.

Both illusions and ambiguous figures suggest that perception is an active process **a**. This offers support for Gregory's theory of perception because this approach argues that our brain actively tries to interpret incoming information **b**. Studies into ambiguous figures (like Rubin's vase) show that we can be led to expect a particular figure and perceive a vase, say, because we have seen pictures of vases beforehand **a**. Again, this supports the idea of perception as an active process, as we can be 'set' to perceive one thing rather than another **b**.

A criticism of the research that is done into illusions is that they are often carried out in artificial situations and therefore lack ecological validity **b**. Such findings may tell us nothing about how perception works in the real world. In fact, illusions in the real world are rare and much of the time our perception is accurate **b**. For example, we normally estimate automatically the distance and speed of objects with accuracy.

e 10/10 marks awarded **(AO1 = 5, AO2 = 5).** This is an excellent answer. It outlines clearly the nature of a visual illusion and gives a good example, and it does the same for an ambiguous figure. **a** This knowledge gains AO1 credit. The student then effectively answers the question set by discussing what these illusions and figures tell us about the active nature of perception. Further AO1 credit is gained from the concept of perception as an active process and for the idea of perceptual set, as well as for knowledge of how a study could manipulate perceptual set. **b** The answer then points out how perception as an active process supports Gregory's theory and why, for which the student gains AO2 credit. The criticism concerning the artificial environment is a valid one and is followed up by a discussion of visual illusions in the real world, which deserves AO2 credit. The student has made an excellent attempt to answer quite a tricky question without giving any irrelevant material. This answer is knowledgeable at the descriptive level, and the discussion contains the necessary level of analysis and evaluation to gain full marks.

Total for this question: 20/20 — grade A.

Question 5 **Individual differences**

Anxiety disorders

(a) Name two types of phobia. (2 marks)

ⓔ This is a straightforward question that requires two names only. There is no reason to go beyond simply stating two of the three named phobias on the specification. Alternatively, named specific phobias (e.g. arachnophobia — phobia of spiders) would be acceptable.

(b) Katy constantly worries about germs. Each time she touches a door handle, she has to wash her hands immediately or she becomes extremely anxious and starts to panic. Her doctor thinks that Katy is suffering from obsessive-compulsive disorder and says that she is to see a specialist.

(i) With reference to Katy, explain what is meant by *obsessions* and *compulsions*. (4 marks)

(ii) Briefly discuss a biological explanation for Katy's obsessive-compulsive disorder. (4 marks)

ⓔ In part (i), an important aspect of the question is the reference to Katy. You should outline what is meant by each term and then link each aspect of the disorder to Katy's behaviour. There would be 1 mark for an accurate brief outline of each term and a second mark for the link to Katy in each case. In part (ii), you can choose any aspect of a biological explanation for OCD, but you must make at least two relevant points that describe this approach. As the question states 'discuss', some of the marks are for evaluation or analysis. These are most likely to be gained by addressing strengths and/or weaknesses of the biological explanation. Alternatively, an analysis of how this explanation might account for Katy's behaviour could gain the AO2 marks.

(c) Discuss *at least one* treatment for phobias. Refer to evidence in your answer. (10 marks)

ⓔ This question requires you to identify at least one treatment for phobias, with half of the marks for knowledge and description of the named treatment and evidence. If you decide to concentrate on one treatment, you must choose one that you know a lot about so that you can gain the full 5 marks. It is important to remember that if you fail to comply with any instruction asking you to refer to evidence, you will gain only a maximum of 6 marks, however good the rest of the answer may be. The marks on such questions can often be more readily accrued by outlining more than one treatment because you would gain straightforward knowledge marks for all relevant and accurate points made for each treatment selected. Probably two treatments would be sufficient. Half of the marks are for evaluation/analysis and these marks can be gained in the following ways: for strengths and weaknesses of the treatments described; for problems in evaluating treatments; for alternative treatments if linked appropriately; for the use of evidence.

Total: 20 marks

Student A

(a) A specific phobia is a phobia where specific things like spiders, lifts, snakes make you very frightened **a**. Another phobia is social situations **b**, some people never go to parties and things because they worry about what other people think of them.

2/2 marks awarded. Here the student **a b** names two appropriate phobias. There was no requirement to go beyond naming them, and indeed it is probably better not to write unnecessarily given the time constraints in the examination. **b** 'Social phobia' would be more accurate for the second type of phobia, but the answer is adequate.

(b) (i) Obsessions are thoughts that are in your mind all the time **a**. You cannot get rid of them and you keep thinking things like 'have I locked the door'. My mum does this all the time and she has to go back and check all the windows and doors every time we go out **b**. It is really annoying and I keep telling her she has OCD.

1/4 marks awarded. a The definition of an obsession is quite good and is worthy of a mark. **b** This student has 'wandered' away from the question and seems to have become embroiled in telling us about his or her mum, forgetting that he or she should be addressing the question. Although a good example of compulsions (checking all the doors) has been given, the student has failed to link this to the term (compulsion) and therefore has not shown that he or she knows that this is compulsive behaviour. In addition, the student has not referred to Katy — as the question asks — and therefore will not gain the application marks. Although the student clearly has some knowledge of obsessive-compulsive behaviour, this knowledge has not been applied to the question.

(ii) A biological explanation for Katy's obsessive behaviour is the genetic explanation **c**. It is probably in her genes because her mum or dad suffers from it. Studies have shown that parents produce children who have OCD if they have it themselves, because you get your genes from your parents. Also brothers and sisters always have it too. This is a good theory because it is biologically proved and studies have been carried out. One study found that if your family has OCD, then there is a 10% chance you will **d**, and people without OCD families are much less likely to get it.

2/4 marks awarded. The student has **c** named an appropriate biological explanation and has offered a rather muddled explanation that nevertheless does get over the idea that family studies have indicated a predisposition to the illness. This would be worthy of a mark. The evaluative point is weak but the **d** results of family studies do point to about a 10% risk of developing OCD if you have relatives with the disorder. This accurate finding, together with the idea that such studies support the genetic explanation, would gain a mark for evaluation/evidence. This student has demonstrated some knowledge (though quite limited), but the communication is poor.

(c) A treatment is systatic desensation **a**. This is a kind of behaviourist treatment and uses classical conditioning. Patients with a spider phobia think of all the situations that make them afraid and then write them down in an order from best to worst **b**. This is known as a higher arc. They then move up from best to worst with the help of the doctor. This is a very quick and effective treatment and is used a lot **c**.

Another treatment is Freud's **d**. His therapy is based on the unconscious because all our worries are in there. He would say patients should relax and say everything that comes into their head, even if it is about sex. When the person is talking freely, defence mechanisms aren't as good and the ego becomes weaker. This means things in the unconscious which are worrying us slip into the conscious and are spoken. Then Freud would listen and tell them what all this means and why they are afraid **e**. This is called free association, which is like word association but different. The trouble with this treatment is it takes a long time and can be quite upsetting for the patient **f**.

e 5/10 marks awarded (AO1 = 4, AO2 = 1). The answer contains some inaccuracies and it does not always use technical terms. However, there is some useful **b e** description and evaluation of two appropriate treatments for phobias. Notice how the student has selected **a d** two treatments, which has worked well because extra marks have been accrued this way. It is likely that the student would not be able to gain as many marks by restricting the answer to one treatment only. The knowledge of two treatments would gain AO1 credit. The **c** evaluative point for the behaviour treatment is vague, not backed up with any evidence and not necessarily correct. This would not gain credit. **f** The evaluation of the psychodynamic treatment is quite valid, encompasses two brief points, and is worthy of credit. As no evidence is presented, the maximum mark that this answer could attain is 6.

Total for this question: 10/20 — approximately grade D.

Student B

(a) Two phobias are: specific phobia, e.g. of spiders **a**, and agoraphobia **b**.

e 2/2 marks awarded. Here the student **a b** names the phobias clearly.

(b) (i) Obsessions are automatic thoughts that keep coming into the mind and that you cannot get rid of unless a particular behaviour is carried out **a**. Katy constantly thinks about germs and worries about contamination, particularly when she touches a door handle, and this worrying is the obsession **b**. **a** A compulsion is a behaviour that the individual feels compelled to perform to relieve the obsessive thoughts. **b** Katy has an overwhelming compulsion to wash her hands and if she does not carry out this compulsion she gets anxious and panicky. This is typical of someone suffering from OCD.

e 4/4 marks awarded. Both terms are clearly **a** explained using correct terminology and both are **b** linked precisely to the case of Katy.

(ii) A biological explanation for Katy's obsessive-compulsive disorder is genetics **c**. Researchers study families to see if there is prevalence of a specific disorder within families. Of course, families share similar genes and the closer you are related to someone the closer the genetic similarity **c**. Thus, identical twins have identical genes, and siblings/non-identical twins share 50% of the same genetic make-up. A study by Pauls found that more than 10% of patients with OCD also have a relative with the same disorder, which is much higher than the control group with no OCD relatives **c**. These results can be used to support the genetic explanation for OCD **d**. However, one problem with family studies is that families also share the same (or similar) environment **d**. It might be that family members observe each other and imitate behaviour. It is difficult to decide whether the environment or genes cause OCD behaviour **d**.

e **4/4 marks awarded.** **c** The beginning of this discussion into the genetic explanation for OCD sets out the rationale behind concordance studies and shows a good understanding. The study is very brief but the findings are accurate and it is an appropriate study given the context. **d** The evaluation is sufficiently discussed to gain the 2 marks.

(c) The behaviourist approach offers a number of treatments, including systematic desensitisation. Systematic desensitisation (SD) relies on the assumption that two competing emotions cannot exist at the same time, so for example we cannot be both relaxed and fearful **a**. Through a process of gradual introduction to the feared object while in a relaxed state, patients are desensitised from their phobia **a**. They would first be trained to relax and then produce a hierarchy from least feared situation to most feared situation regarding their phobia. A person with a phobia of moths might have as the least feared 'looking at a picture of a moth' and the most feared 'actually holding a moth' **a**. Patients in a relaxed state are introduced to the least feared situation and gradually work up the hierarchy while remaining relaxed (and therefore not anxious).

An alternative way of treating phobias is with psychodynamic therapy. This involves accessing the unconscious because it is thought things that cause us anxiety are locked into the unconscious **b**. The ego defence mechanisms that are in place to protect from anxiety have to be lifted. This can be done by free association where the patient relaxes and says out loud everything in the mind **b**. The ego begins to have difficulty managing the unconscious id impulses, which begin to slip through and can be interpreted by the analyst. However, the analysis of the unconscious can prove traumatic for patients as, when the defence mechanisms are lifted, negative emotions such as guilt are released **c**.

Systematic desensitisation is a well focused method and is much more effective than other long-term methods such as psychoanalytic therapy **d**. SD works well in the therapeutic situation but it does not always generalise to real life **d**. When the patient returns to their everyday life, the phobia can resume, although Lang and Lazovik showed improvement with snake phobia continued six months after treatment. It is also only suitable where a specific object or situation can be identified **d**. It cannot really be applied to more general phobias such as social phobias. Overall, studies have shown that behaviour therapy is just as or even more effective than other therapies, such as psychodynamic therapy **d**.

e **10/10 marks awarded (AO1= 5, AO2 = 5).** This is a thorough answer with several creditworthy **a** descriptive points in the first paragraph, particularly for systematic desensitisation. **a** The rationale behind systematic desensitisation has been outlined clearly and the descriptions of the treatments are accurate. **a** The use of the example (moth) is appropriate and helps to clarify the explanation given. **b** The knowledge and understanding of treatments required for the AO1 credit is evident. **c d** The evaluation of the treatments is also quite thorough and a discussion of the points is evident, as demonstrated in the examples of the types of phobia not suited to SD and what is meant by 'it does not always generalise to real life'. **d** Although the last point about the efficacy of behaviour therapy over other therapies is only mentioned briefly, the alternative therapy has been explained earlier and it is an appropriate one. Taken as a whole, this answer provides an accurate description of two approaches to therapy and includes some well-argued evaluation and analysis. Although the reference to evidence is very brief, the student does meet that criterion.

Total for this question: 20/20 — grade A.

Question 6 **Individual differences**

Autism

(a) Researchers have noted that children with autism do not engage in joint attention. Use an example to explain what is meant by *joint attention.* (3 marks)

e This question is asking you to do two things: demonstrate your knowledge of joint attention and link your explanation to an example. First, you have to state what 'joint attention' means exactly. Second, you need to give an example relating to the term that will help to explain it clearly. If no example is given, the full marks cannot be attained.

(b) Joe is a 5-year-old boy who has recently been diagnosed with autism. He hardly ever looks at other people and rarely communicates. When he does speak, it is difficult to understand what he is trying to say and he often repeats the same sound over and over again.

(i) Outline how the Lovaas technique might be used to help Joe's language development. (3 marks)

(ii) Briefly discuss parental involvement in therapeutic programmes with autistic children like Joe. (4 marks)

e Before the questions, there is a text about Joe indicating some of the language difficulties that have contributed to his recent diagnosis of autism. This information should be read carefully because it contains important details that can be used in your answer. For example, Joe's speech is unclear. You should use this information in your answer to question (i) to indicate how the Lovaas technique could be applied to improve Joe's language development. This question requires you to link to Joe, although knowledge of the Lovaas technique should be outlined and applied accurately first and foremost. In part (ii), parental involvement is a particular topic on the specification and it really concerns a discussion of how important the adult carers are to the efficacy of the treatment programme. Note that this question states 'discuss', meaning that some analysis/evaluation is required. The discussion could be in the form of studies that have assessed how important parental involvement is to the continued improvement in children with autism.

(c) Describe and evaluate *at least one* biological explanation of autism. Refer to evidence in your answer. (10 marks)

e You are expected to show your knowledge of at least one biological approach to explaining autism. Questions that ask for 'at least one' can often gain marks more readily by referring to more than one. This is because to gain the full 5 marks for one explanation, a thorough description and knowledge of that one theory is needed. (However, it should be noted that some knowledge marks, usually 1 or 2, can be gained from the description of studies.) Remember, it is always important to use any specialist terminology, as it shows that you have been studying the topic. Half of the marks in these straightforward extended writing questions are for knowledge and description. The remaining marks are for evaluation, i.e. presenting strengths and limitations and using evidence to support what you say. In this question, you are also required to 'refer to evidence in your answer'. It is important to remember that if you fail to comply with this instruction, you will gain only a maximum of 6 marks, however good the rest of the answer may be.

Total: 20 marks

Student A

(a) Joint attention is where the mother and baby both look at the same thing, for example a toy **a**.

e **0/2 marks awarded.** Here the student **a** almost defines joint attention, but does not quite capture the most essential part of the definition, i.e. that it involves a shared interaction: the mother and child are not simply looking at an object but also looking at each other in such a way that they are sharing the experience and emotion.

(b) (i) Lovaas used a behavioural technique based on ABC **a**. A is for? and is where a request is made of Joe, e.g. choose a book Joe **b**. B is for behaviour from Joe. If he chooses a book then this will be rewarded. This is known as reinforcement and behaviourists use it to encourage the behaviour they want **b**.

e **2/3 marks awarded.** The student clearly has forgotten some of the terms in this answer, such as 'antecedent'. However, he or she correctly explains some of the **a** essential components of the Lovaas technique. It is a behavioural technique and **b** the example illustrates how it might be applied to Joe, along with the essential notion that **b** reinforcement is an element of this technique. As the student does not mention language, it is not a complete answer to the question set.

(ii) Parental involvement in therapeutic programmes with autistic children like Joe is good. Parents are important because they can encourage children when they are at home **c**. If the parents are interested then the child will probably get better at things. Studies have shown that just 30 hours of parents working with their child proves better than over 200 hours with a doctor **d**.

e **2/4 marks awarded.** The first sentence is entirely redundant because it practically repeats the question. **c** In the second sentence, the student shows some understanding that parental involvement is important for the continued efficacy of treatment and this is worthy of an AO1 mark. **d** The student has tried to back up the point with some evidence and although it is a little vague, the numbers have been accurately remembered from a study by Koegel. (In any case, essentially studies have indeed indicated the superiority of parental involvement.) This is worthy of an AO2 mark. Although this answer is brief, it does make an important point and backs this up.

(c) A biological explanation for autism is that it is due to genes because if a member of your family has autism it is much more likely that you will have it too **a**. In fact evidence shows that you are up to ten times more likely to have autism if a person in your family has it **b**. Autism is also more likely to occur in boys than girls, which suggests a genetic reason **c**. Both family and twin studies have been carried out to see if there is a correlation in autism **d**. Identical twins have identical genes and so if one twin has autism and the disorder is due to genes, then you would expect the other twin to have it — in other words there will be a correlation. A number of studies have found this to be the case. In fact a study by? on DZ and MZ twins showed a much higher rate of correlation in DZ twins, which are identical twins **e**. One of the problems with this kind of research, however, is that if it was just due to genes then 100% should match and so the social must also be important **f**. Another criticism of the genetic findings is that approximately 20% of non-identical twins have autism if the other twin has **g**. They are no closer than brothers and so should only be 2%, unless the environment, which is similar for twins, has effect.

e **6/10 marks awarded (AO1 = 3, AO2 = 3).** The answer is short but the student does seem to have some basic idea about the genetic nature of autism and there is some evidence to back up the discussion. **a** The idea that autism is much more prevalent in families where there is another person with autism is worthy of AO1 credit (knowledge). **b** This is backed up with the evidence of 'ten times more likely', which is an accurate figure and worthy of AO2 credit. **c** The higher incidence of autism in boys and the implication of genetic influences is another valid AO1 point, **d** as is the information on twin studies being used to research concordance. **e** The discussion of MZ and DZ twins is confused: there is an error (MZ, not DZ, twins are identical) and the studies and conclusions are not well explained. However, the point about the **f** lack of 100% concordance is worthy of evaluation (AO2) credit. **g** The final point is a little clumsy but it does gain evaluation credit because what the student is trying to say is evident and it is a valid point.

Total for this question: 10/20 — approximately grade D.

Student B

(a) When a parent and child (about 18 months) look at something together, joint attention can occur **a** and this is where the mother and baby both look at the same thing and then look at each other, as though they are sharing the experience **b**. The child will often look at the parent and then back to the object. For example, if a child sees a dog he or she might point to the dog and then look at the parent to share the experience and joy **c**. The parent can then respond and say something like 'Yes, that is a beautiful dog, shall we go and stroke it?' Although the child does not understand the words, he or she will probably smile and join in the communication. This joint attention does not occur with autistic children.

e **3/3 marks awarded.** Here the student **a** defines joint attention thoroughly and does capture the most essential part of the definition, i.e. **b** that it involves a shared interaction: the mother and child are not simply looking at an object, but also looking at each other in such a way that they are sharing the experience and emotion. This answer uses an **c** appropriate example to explain the concept.

(b) (i) Lovaas used a behavioural technique called discrete trial training or DTT **a**. This is based on the A (**a**ntecedent), B (**b**ehaviour) and C (**c**onsequence) model. With Joe, a request would be made (the A), e.g. to choose a piece of the jigsaw puzzle **b**. B is for behaviour from Joe. If he chooses a piece of jigsaw, this will be reinforced with a positive comment such as 'Well done Joe, that is a corner piece and we know where that goes, don't we?' **c** This reward is used to encourage the behaviour that is required.

e 2/3 marks awarded. The student has outlined the Lovaas technique that could be used with Joe and correctly explains some of the **a** essential components of the Lovaas technique. It is identified as a behavioural technique, which is worth a mark. **b** The example illustrates how the technique might be applied to Joe, and the essential notion that **c** reinforcement is an element of the technique is appropriately given. Unfortunately, the student does not make any reference to language as the question requires.

(ii) Studies have shown that parental involvement in therapeutic programmes with autistic children like Joe is necessary if the gains from therapy are to continue after the programme has finished **d**. Parents encourage children when they are at home to continue with the appropriate behaviour by rewarding good behaviour and not reinforcing poor behaviour **e**. However, there are problems of this reliance on parental involvement, because the involvement is lengthy and time-consuming, and some parents are just not able to invest that time **f**. Also, if such time is invested in one member of the family, other family members may suffer **g**.

e 4/4 marks awarded. The student shows good understanding that parental involvement is important for the continued efficacy of treatment. **d e** The first two sentences show accurate knowledge about the necessity of parental involvement and are worthy of 2 AO1 marks. **f** The student has then made an important critical analysis of this parental involvement, **g** the final sentence being a valid expansion of this (2 AO2 points).

(c) There are a number of biological explanations for autism, including neurological correlates and genetics **a**. Neuroimaging studies, such as those that used PET, have pointed to a number of areas of the brain in autistic individuals that seem different from those in a normal brain **a**. For example, abnormality in the frontal cortex of autistic children has been found in studies. However, PET is not widely used with children because it requires the injection of radiation into the blood stream and the child has to undergo a number of blood analyses, meaning that samples have to be taken **b**.

Another biological explanation for autism is that it is due to genetic influences, and findings have shown that if a member of your family has autism it is much more likely that you will have it too **a**. Evidence shows that you are up to ten times more likely to have autism if a person in your family has the condition. Autism is also more likely to occur in boys than girls, and this suggests a genetic influence in autism **a**. Both family and twin studies have been carried out to see if there is a higher concordance of autism in family members who are more similar genetically **a**. Identical twins have identical genes and so if one twin has autism and the disorder is due to genes, then you would expect the other twin to have an increased risk of autism also. A number of studies have found this to be the case. A study by Rutter (1977) found that concordance rates for MZ twins both of whom are on the autistic spectrum were as high as 90% **a**. One of the criticisms of concordance studies is that they fail to unravel the effect of nature and nurture **b**. If autism was purely genetic, there should be 100% concordance, i.e. if one MZ twin has autism then the other should also develop the condition, yet this is not the case. Another criticism of the genetic findings is that there is approximately 20% concordance for DZ or non-identical twins and as they are no more alike than ordinary siblings there is no genetic reason why this concordance rate should be so much higher than the average 2% found for ordinary siblings **b**. This leads to the conclusion that nurture, or the environment, must also have an influence on the development of autism **b**.

e 10/10 marks awarded **(AO1 = 5, AO2 = 5).** This is a thorough answer. The student chooses to discuss both **a** neurological correlates and genetics, and by so doing accesses all the AO1 credit. The knowledge of these biological explanations is both accurate and substantial, especially for **a** genetics. The evaluative comments are also excellent. **b** There is accurate and appropriate use of research, and a solid **b** understanding of the nature–nurture debate with respect to autism is conveyed. This answer goes beyond what is strictly necessary for a top-band answer, but is indicative of the kind of answer given by exceptional students.

Total for this question: 19/20 — grade A.

Knowledge check answers

Social influence

1 If a person is skilled at a task then the dominant response will be to perform well, i.e. performance will be facilitated. On a new skill, the dominant response will be to perform badly and performance on a task will be hindered.

2 Any relevant example, e.g. when I had to carry out a presentation in assembly I was nervous and worried about what my peers would think of me and this affected my performance because I did it perfectly when practising at home but forgot many of the things I wanted to say in the actual assembly. My performance was inhibited due to evaluation apprehension.

3 Any example, e.g. compliance would be agreeing with my friends that organic food is better for you (although privately still thinking that there was no real benefit to organic food), whereas internalisation would be agreeing with my friends that organic food is better for you (and privately thinking that there was a real benefit to organic food).

4 Task difficulty — on a more difficult task, conformity levels increase. No unanimity — if at least one other person does not conform then you have an ally and are less likely to conform yourself, and conformity decreases.

5 The authoritarian personality type is associated with increased obedience in an individual. This type of personality is rigid and blindly obedient to authority.

Social cognition

6 Kelley used a real person — a guest lecturer in his study, which is more true to life than simply giving people a list of adjectives that describe a person, which is what occurred in the Asch study.

7 Dispositional attributions are explanations concerning the person, some trait within the individual, whereas situational attributions are not to do with the person, but are factors in the environment.

8 Three structural components of attitudes are: affective, behavioural and cognitive.

9 This is probably serving an adaptive function because the attitude will achieve rewards and lead to the desired place at medical school.

10 Any two relevant groups, for example, my drama group and the three close friends who form my peer friendship group.

Remembering and forgetting

11 Maintenance rehearsal is simply repeating the words, similar to the rehearsal process in the multi-store model of memory. Elaborative rehearsal involves going over the material by processing the meaning and not simply repeating. Maintenance rehearsal results in longer-lasting memory.

12 I had egg and bacon for breakfast this morning.

13 It might be the distracter task that is causing the forgetting and not simply the passage of time. The distracter task might act as an interference.

14 Appropriate retrieval cues might not be available in the examination, particularly if you revised in your bedroom, which is quite a different context from the examination room, so you might not recall information in the examination.

15 This is a study that is carried out in the natural environment where the behaviour is usually found.

16 Repressed memories might result in anxiety disorders, with the conscious focus of anxiety merely symbolising the repressed fear.

Perceptual processes

17 Perceptual set is an unconscious bias towards perceiving things in a certain way. For example, if you have recently bought a red VW Golf car then you begin to notice all the same cars on the road.

18 The control group acted as a comparison so that any differences in ratings could be assessed as due to the hunger and not some other variable.

19 Young children's drawing would lack perspective, as this would take time to practise and learn.

20 Similarity, proximity, closure.

21 Convergence, and retinal disparity.

22 Size constancy would allow us to perceive the bird as the correct size because it would take account not just of the size on the retinal image but would also take account of the distance. Taking account of the distance we would use constancy scaling to mentally enlarge our perception of the bird to normal size.

23 (i) Gregory's theory is top-down — expectations in the brain work downwards to influence the way we interpret the sensory information from a stimulus, whereas Gibson's theory is bottom-up — perception starts with sensory input from the object to the retina and is then interpreted by the brain. (ii) Gregory's theory can explain perceptual errors (e.g. the Müller-Lyer illusion) whereas Gibson's theory cannot explain visual illusions.

Anxiety disorders

24 (i) Phobias are extreme fears that are disproportionate to the danger posed. (ii) Specific phobia e.g. snakes; social phobia e.g. public speaking; agoraphobia e.g. fear of open spaces.

25 It was a loud bang.

26 When the interviews have taken place and the materials collated, the interviewer then has to interpret the material and it is difficult to do this in an objective way. For example, the researcher may be biased towards interpreting material to fit in with a pre-existing theory.

27 Identical twins who are separated at birth and brought up in different environments could be investigated. If there is a high concordance rate for OCD, in spite of the different environments, then it is likely that there is a genetic influence.

28 One thought might be: 'Did I check the bathroom window? Did I turn the handle both ways? If I don't check again a burglar might ransack my home and I will be out on the street.' A counterstatement might be: 'You have already checked all windows and, think about it, the window gap is too small for a person and it is impossible to access that window from the outside.'

Autism

29 (i) Impairment in social interaction, for example poor use of eye-gaze and gestures. (ii) Impairment in communication, for example a delay in the acquisition of language and speech.

30 Autism is considered a 'syndrome' because a set of symptoms occurs together (poor social interaction, poor communication and repetitive behaviour) that appear to have a common origin.

31 Because both twins and autism are rare, then samples are very small and therefore not necessarily representative of the wider population. This makes generalising from such small samples less reliable.

32 Four years old.

33 The control group acts as a comparison so that it can be assessed whether the therapy was effective or whether such changes would have occurred over time anyway.

34 If parents are involved in the therapeutic programme they can continue with the therapy in their natural home environments and ensure that the improvement generalises to everyday contexts.

Index